"Jason Greer's experiences and maturity teach us a lot about the way our lives should be lived."

—TONY HALL, United States Ambassador, Nobel Peace Prize nominee, and author, *Changing the Face of Hunger.*

"As a mother, I have often yearned to see my children's lives through their eyes. *Very Much Better* is just that opportunity—to see through a son's eyes as he faces cancer with faith, doubt, family—and some of the most heroic friends in recent literature. Every mother should experience this book."

—ELKE GOVERTSEN, publisher, *Mamalode* Magazine.

"*Very Much Better* is a window into a world that none of us would choose to be in. As filled as it was with pain and loss, we sense that Jason would not change his experience because it led him to a profound understanding of love, courage, family and faith."

—MARY MALLOY, professor of Maritime Studies, and author, *The Wandering Heart* and *Paradise Walk.*

"I cried and I laughed and felt every emotion that I can imagine while I read *Very Much Better.* Jason gives us all an insight into what he and so many other children face as they fight cancer. This is a book everyone should read."

—GOVERNOR JUDY MARTZ, Montana

"*Very Much Better* gives us a child's view of living with cancer and dealing with the unknown. Jason takes us along on his journey and shows us the courage, strength, and even humor that children with cancer carry with them. Even through the worst times, Jason shares his reality with us and how he dealt with all the adult experiences he had to endure before his time and how his family helped him in the process."

—MICHELE ASHBY, President and Founder, Dani's Foundation, Denver, CO.

Very Much Better

A Cancer Memoir by a Boy Who Lived

Jason Paul Greer

ISBN 978-0-87842-694-2

M&M's® is a registered trademark of Mars, Inc., all rights reserved.
CHEETOS® is a registered trademark of Frito-Lay North America, Inc., all rights reserved.
Velcro® is a registered trademark of Velcro USA Inc.

Copyright 2012 by Jason Paul Greer
Printed in the USA
All rights reserved

This book may not be reproduced in whole or in part by electronic or any other means which exist or may yet be developed, without permission of:

Second Printing:

Mountain Press Publishing Company
Phone: (406) 728-1900
Toll Free: 800-234-5308
www.mountain-press.com

Limit of Liability/Disclaimer of Warranty: While the publisher and the author have used their best efforts in preparing this book, they make no representations or warranties with respect to the accuracy or completeness of the contents of this book and specifically disclaim any implied warranties of merchantability or fitness for a particular purpose. No warranty may be created or extended by sales representatives or written sales materials. The advice and strategies contained herein may not be suitable for your situation. You should consult with a professional where appropriate. Neither the publisher nor the author shall be liable for any loss of profit or any other commercial damages, including but not limited to special, incidental, consequential, or other damages.

To Chad, Erik and Jesse.

Up to 90 percent of the author's proceeds from the sale of this book will be dedicated to helping young people facing difficulty, and to help find a cure for cancer, so we might finally silence a piper that has stolen too many of our children.

Acknowledgments

A special thanks is included below.

First, to those who shaped the story:

> My parents, brother, grandparents, aunts, uncles, cousins, and to my sweet wife Emily—our adventure goes on. Bill and Cherié, the Tesarik family, and the Schuette family—for your kindness, love and support.

And to those that made this book a reality:

> Mary Malloy and Tricia Brown—without your encouragement, mentorship and all-around faith in me, this book would not have been possible. The entire staff at ACS Publishing—for taking a risk, and sticking with a first-time writer.

Table of Contents

xiii	Prologue
1	Chapter 1: Spring Fever
9	Chapter 2: Small Surgery Called a Biopsy
15	Chapter 3: Bicycles, Baseball Cards, Oncology, and Chemotherapy
21	Chapter 4: Send Off
27	Chapter 5: A Thousand Zip Codes from Home
31	Chapter 6: IV Stand, Skateboards, and Prosthetic Leg Sword Fights
37	Chapter 7: Bones from a Cadaver
43	Chapter 8: The Art of Throwing Up
49	Chapter 9: A Wish is Granted
55	Chapter 10: Grateful Travis
59	Chapter 11: McDonald House Breakfast Club
67	Chapter 12: Bald by Eleven
73	Chapter 13: The Chemo Cut
77	Chapter 14: Memories of Home
81	Chapter 15: The Cancer Patient's Guide to Duct Tape
85	Chapter 16: Questions for God
91	Chapter 17: Lucky to Have Cancer?
93	Chapter 18: Black Eyes, Bloody Lip, and a Bald Head

99	Chapter 19: Home for a Visit
105	Chapter 20: You're Gonna Make It
109	Chapter 21: Death Came to Stay
115	Chapter 22: Communion of Suffering
119	Chapter 23: Boys' Bathrooms aren't Pink
123	Chapter 24: Fought the Good Fight, Finished the Race, Kept the Faith
129	Chapter 25: Traveling to Russia, Returning to Serve
137	Chapter 26: A Young Lady, Different from the Rest
151	Chapter 27: Lighting Strikes, Church Bells Ring, and Our Girl Says Good-bye
159	*Epilogue*
169	*Letters to Heaven*
177	*Resources*

Prologue

"Why are your eyes sad?" she asked, reaching up with her tiny right hand and pressing it against the whiskers on my face.

Stunned by her question, I looked down at this child of four. Her hair was dark, full of curls, and just long enough to fit into pigtails. Barrettes in her hair were the same color as her pink dress. Her skin was tanned by summer sun, and she appeared healthy. Dark circles beneath her brown eyes were the only subtle indication that she had been sick, recently completing her final chemotherapy treatment.

Ice cream dripped from the little girl's chin and ran down the hand holding what was left of a two-scoop vanilla cone—a smile stretched across her young face. We sat in the grass on a green hillside overlooking the Pacific Northwest's Puget Sound, in a place not far from Children's Hospital, where at different times both this little girl and I were treated for cancer.

My companion on the hillside was one of several children afflicted with cancer who were given the experience of a summer camp away from hospitals, doctors, and cancer treatments. It was a week of campfires and dining-hall food, swimming and playing.

As I transitioned from camp counselor to a director of this camp, I inevitably spent more time planning and managing, and less beside a child. However, a lull in the day had afforded me the opportunity to sit in the grass and enjoy the company of a little girl who had overcome cancer, and been free of the disease for the past few months. The sun melted my two scoops of vanilla quicker than I could get them down, and I smiled in return as ice cream dripped onto my hand.

My smile caused her question to surprise me all the more. My smile was not a front. I was happy. But when closely examined, my expression captured the delight and sadness that simultaneously arose from being part of a summer camp filled with children suffering from cancer.

"*Why are your eyes sad?*" This question stayed with me.

I should not have been surprised. Most of the wisdom gathered in my life did not come from veterans of many years, but from the innocence and simplicity of youth. Then again, it might be impossible to get used to the sterling reflections that sometimes spring from children. This child's wise question immediately caused memories to pile up in my mind. I choked on thoughts of the past, and could make no reply. In a moment, flashes of sickness, health, joy, loss, and laughter silently pressed against me, and I remembered a story: a story that strengthened both the smile on my face and sadness in my eyes. It began when I was eleven years old and was diagnosed with cancer.

In 1991, a doctor first told me I suffered from a rare bone cancer called Ewing's Sarcoma, and still the clearest way to tell this story is to write down the memories as seen through my eyes when I was a child. I do not write with the alchemy that enables the gifted writer to turn any letter, word, or sentence into something shining and beautiful. This story was crafted with a divine hand long before I was born, and beautiful long before I resolved to tell it. And though I tell the story, it is about much more than me. If I were to write only about myself, I would have nothing to tell, and no one to tell my *nothing* to. It is not who I am or even my fight against cancer that sets this story apart from others. It is those I have walked beside who mark my life with amazement. I am an understudy, an observer fortunate enough to encounter a few of those rare people who know what it is to live.

I do not have clear answers for many of the questions I wondered about as a boy. However, along with telling the story just as I remember it, looking back through my own childhood eyes, I have also included a parallel voice—my current thoughts regarding cancer. The narration contains lyrics of raw emotion and reflection, unpolished convictions I cannot get past or overlook—convictions I do not pretend to totally understand, or have the ability to articulate perfectly, but are as certain as my faith, family, and the changing seasons.

Chapter One

Spring Fever

By the time I was eleven, I'd already said lots of prayers. Just the usual: thanking God for the food, Mom and Dad, friends, and for my brother every once in a while. For help in school, and to help starving kids in countries far, far away. That's not even counting saying sorry for cursing. But for the first time in my life, I really needed to pray. I was scared right down to my toes, and I needed God to help keep me safe, even if it was supposed to be just a small surgery, something the doctors called a "biopsy."

God…please take care of me.

The nurse pushed my hospital bed down a narrow hallway.

As we approached the operating room, the busy sounds of Saint Patrick's Hospital softened, and the squeak of the bed's wheels became louder.

Walking beside me, Mom and Dad each held one of my hands. But when we all reached the operating room's two big doors, they couldn't go any further. I was pushed through the doors, and Mom and Dad had to let go, leaving me in the hands of hospital staff.

Turning my head and looking back, I strained to see my parents. Dad's jaw clinched and Mom looked worried, but neither one was crying. I knew they were stumped, confused about how to feel, emotions headed in opposite directions. Of course, Mom and Dad were scared because I was being operated on, but they wanted answers that could come only from this biopsy. After surgery, my parents hoped I'd be wheeled out of the operating room, perfectly healthy and back to my old self again.

The doors closed automatically, and I was sealed inside a cold, white room. A doctor introduced himself as the anesthesiologist. He spoke to me delicately about school and sports, as if he didn't want to wake anyone.

"What grade are you in, Jason?" whispered the doctor, dressed in soft blue from top to bottom.

"Fifth," I answered.

"Play any sports?" he continued.

"Yeah," I said quietly.

"Which ones?"

"Probably, all of 'em."

"And do you have a girlfriend?" asked a blonde lady, a nurse, now standing next to the doctor.

I smiled, rolled my eyes, and looked away. No answer.

The night before surgery, Dad had told me all about anesthesiologists and bet me I couldn't count to ten once they gave me the anesthetic. I'd taken the bet, and my fists were clenched and palms sweating when the doctor finally told me I could begin counting.

"One." Heart beating in my ears, I looked above me at the white ceiling, then to the white walls, while a dry, medicine cabinet kind of smell nearly made me gag.

"Two." My skin was cold, covered with goose bumps and uncomfortably damp with sweat. I'd never been so scared before, not even over the past few weeks when I'd gone from examination to examination. This surgery was small, and I didn't even need to stay in the hospital overnight. But lying in a cold room, knowing I was being put under and about to be operated on...

"Three." I was afraid of the surgery itself, not its results. *Will it hurt? Will I be sick? When will I wake up?*

"Four." I looked to my left. Out of the corner of my eye, I could see the odd bump that'd caused Mom to worry and doctors to wonder. I remembered looking in the mirror weeks before, noticing the bump on the top of my left collarbone for the first time.

Stupid bump, a spiteful thought flashed.

It was small then, about the size of a green pea. It hurt if I pushed on it, so I didn't, and I got along fine. I didn't think about it again until one day when I was playing football after school.

"Five." Some of my favorite times happened on evenings just like the one when my bump became a problem. After the final school bell, kids from our neighborhood would finish after-school snacks and meet in the street for a game of home-run derby or street football. We played in all seasons and conditions, fall, winter, rain or shine. But spring evenings in Montana were best. The weather was warm enough to show us kids that summer was on its way, but it was still cold enough to remind us that winter didn't want to give up and leave.

Short-sleeved T-shirts replaced winter coats, and the street football game went on from the time we finished school until the sun set on Hellgate Canyon and on the mountains that made up our backdrop. During the football game, another player accidently hit the bump on my shoulder. The pain was fierce, and I fell to my knees in tears.

"Six." I remembered Mom's face when I showed her the bump. She was worried, and her reaction led to a series of doctor's appointments and medical exams.

"Seven." I said quietly. I thought about how fast the bump had grown. In a few short weeks it had gone from the size of a pea to a golf ball. I closed my eyes and remembered the day my friend Matthew and I cut school—the same day that Dr. Susa had told me I needed to have this biopsy.

"Eight." Anesthetic warmed my blood, and I felt like the bed was slowly sinking through the floor.

"Nine..."

* * * * *

A Look Back: Postage for all Time and Space

"*Hold on tight, kid.*"

That is what I would say if I could reach back and speak to the child I was. These are the words I would write if I could pass advice to the younger version of myself through H.G. Wells' time machine, or if I could give a letter to God as he conducts time, moving in and out of years as he pleases.

Life would be different if we could write a thoughtful letter and have it delivered to a time past or maybe even to heaven. Life would be different if we could spell out sappy clichés that, regrettably, we did not have the courage to say to a loved one when we had the chance. But that is not the design of life.

If I could draft a letter to the child I was, it would be sent to the moment in my life just before the biopsy and my diagnosis with bone cancer. And yet, even if I could magically pass advice across time, I would not tell myself everything.

If I had only facts, there would be no surprise, no magic, or miracles—there would be only fact. I suppose this is how a father feels when he gives a child space and permits him to struggle, allowing success and experience to be the child's. I imagine this is why God allows us choices even though our choices are often wrong; this is possibly even why God leaves much of his divine plans unseen, requiring mankind to have faith and believe.

However, if miraculously given the chance, I would love to tell my younger version a few things. I would tell that fifth-grade boy, nervous about being in an operating room and having surgery, that he has cancer and facing his disease will be like standing in a terrible storm. I would try to make him understand that the experiences roaring toward him are untamable, unstoppable, and that Mom and Dad will not be able to shelter him.

He would know that making it through this storm requires a fight. He would never choose this, but his fight will be a cornerstone in forming the man he will become. If I didn't think it would frighten an eleven-year-old even more, I would tell him the fear of being operated on for the first time is simply the beginning, and is not worth worrying about. "Enjoy the life you've known for eleven years. It's brilliant and it will only last a second longer!" I might say. But most of all, if I was only allowed a moment, I would tell him to "Hold on tight."

* * * * *

Cutting school wasn't easy. Matthew and I knew that the lady who ran the school's administrative office wouldn't let us go without questions.

"What's her name, Mrs…who?" I whispered, just steps from the grade school's office and principal.

"I don't know," he replied, "I always call her the Office Lady."

"Lot of good that does," I said.

Matthew helped me change a note Dad had written in pencil days before. The note had let my fifth-grade teacher and the Office Lady know I needed to be excused from school so I could see a doctor. A few simple changes to the note, and the afternoon wouldn't be spent in my fifth-grade classroom or in a doctor's office, but outside, away from parents, teachers, and doctors.

My penmanship was much too terrible to pass for my father's, so Matthew changed the date to read, "*April 5, 1991,*" and right after the words, "*Please excuse*

Jason," Mathew drew an arrow to the note's margin and wrote, "and Matthew." He added his mother's signature to the bottom.

The Office Lady leaned her head over a tall counter and looked down at us. She had a beehive hairdo. Her eyes were magnified by her thick glasses. She looked at the note, holding it out away from her, straightening her arm and squinting.

I shoved Matthew forward, toward what I guessed was her line of sight. He had a mop of blond hair, and a funny charm that made every girl in school give him at least one heart-shaped valentine a year, and sometimes two. My cheek was a little bruised and my nose a bit swollen from a punch I took during morning recess a day earlier. I was sure Matthew looked less guilty than I.

But this woman—falling somewhere between sixty and seventy years old, between a teacher and a principal, between a school intercom switch and a well-deserved retirement—didn't look at Matthew. She looked right at me, and I suddenly was sure the afternoon was going to be spent in detention, not riding our bicycles to the river, catching snakes, and skipping rocks.

"More tests today, Jason?" asked the women behind the tall desk.

"Yes, ma'am," I answered.

Her eyebrows rose as she read further. Matthew and I each took a deep breath and offered an innocent smile that we'd practiced before walking to the office.

"You're bringing a friend to the doctor?" she asked.

"Yes, ma'am…ummm…for support…ya' know?" I answered, wiping my nose with the back of my hand, then wiping my hand on my blue jeans.

My heart pounded harder as she carefully looked over the note.

"Good luck," she said. "I'll let your teacher know why you two are absent."

Matthew and I turned and started to leave. Excitement, nervousness, all bottled up inside us while standing in front of the Office Lady, wanted to burst out and we wanted to run through the school doors. But both of us knew it was important to walk slowly and play it cool until out of sight.

Both Matthew and I lived in the center of Missoula, on the valley floor or the "flats," as we called it. Our houses weren't as nice as those up on the hills. But we had a straight shot, with nothing to climb, and could ride our bicycles all over town. In a matter of minutes, we could pedal to the edge of a river, which bordered mountains and wilderness that beckoned us to explore.

It was the feeling of freedom: hours without somebody telling us what to do, a well-working bicycle, and a town we could ride across in about a half-hour. Matthew and I leisurely pedaled our bikes on a road that was part pavement and part dirt. I always took this particular road when I cut school. It was the long way, leading me around the outskirts of Missoula, and letting me ride right next to a mountain.

I took the long way partially because I thought fewer people might see me and I'd be less likely to get caught cutting school, and partially so I'd be beside something as big as a mountain. The mountains were the only skyscrapers within five hundred miles, and I liked being next to them. Their size made whatever trouble I'd caused seem unimportant.

Matthew and I leaned our bikes against an old pine tree near the road and walked along a muddy trail. We followed it through some brush and down a steep hill to a bend in the Clark Fork River. The afternoon was spent running the riverbank. We

Spring Fever

flipped over large rocks, scrambling after snakes as they slithered away, and skipped small, flat stones off the ripples in the river's current.

In my opinion, Missoula is the best part of Western Montana. We lived in a valley, surrounded by the Rocky Mountains. Forests, peaks, foothills, and rivers inspired local people to spend time in the outdoors. Missoula was even a setting for books and movies, like Norman Maclean's *A River Runs Through It*.

My family's experiences in the outdoors were different than popular scenes of casting a fly rod. My favorite fishing tackle had nothing to do with fly-fishing. I enjoyed using worms and a bright orange fishing pole with a picture of Snoopy on it. I had little patience and never wanted to take the time to perfect artistic fishing. But more than that, fishing meant something different to me than others in Montana.

If you were to ask Dad about his occupation, he'd likely tell you he was an ordained minister; he might even call himself a youth pastor. He always loved ministry, but it didn't pay very well. So as far back as I could remember, it was Dad's other job as a commercial fisherman in Alaska that paid our bills; I guess I just thought of fishing as work, and usually spent my spare time doing other things.

Still, some of the best fishermen around visited Missoula, and a famous quote described our town as a "junction of great trout rivers": the Blackfoot, Bitterroot, and Clark Fork. While I didn't spend much time fishing these rivers, I swam in the Clark Fork and played on its banks.

By the time Matthew and I got back to the path that led up the hill, our faces were sunburned and red from running. We walked up the muddy trail away from the Clark Fork, to the old pine and our bicycles.

"What was that noise?" Matthew asked, hushed.

He pointed about halfway up the hill toward a rustle in a patch of bushes.

"Dunno…"

The noise might've been caused by a black bear or a mountain lion, but before we had a chance to be alarmed or run away, my big brother came rolling out of the brush, caught in an out-of-control tumble like a big log bouncing down a steep hill. The tumble brought him to the bank and almost into the Clark Fork before his momentum stopped with a painful groan.

"Ouch," he moaned.

Jon sat up and shook his head. He hadn't hurt himself seriously, but he'd skinned his elbow and torn a hole in his blue jeans.

My brother rubbed his arm and looked down at the hole in his jeans.

"Damn! I just got these jeans," he said. "Mom's gonna kill me."

I looked at the hole in his pant leg.

"Not if she finds out what I did today," I mumbled.

"Jon, what happened to you?" Matthew asked my brother.

"I was just waiting to jump out of the bushes and scare ya," he said, "and then something slipped, and I lost my balance."

"It worked. You scared us all right," I said laughing. "Need a hand, klutz?"

Jon nodded as he wiped blood and dirt off his elbow and onto his pants.

It was easy to see that Jon and I were brothers. We both had dark hair and freckled faces. But Jon was two years older, already shaving, and nearly twice my size. Matthew and I each grabbed a hand and pulled Jon to his feet.

The talents God gave my brother puzzled me. This wasn't the first time he'd tried to scare me and ended up end-over-end. Once, I saw him look too long at an airplane while riding his bicycle and run into the back of parked car. But Jon could untie any knot; he could straighten even the most tangled shoelaces. And the second he got to the river, he could find a perfectly flat stone and send it skipping across the water as if that were its whole purpose in life.

I liked regular public school. Jon attended a private Christian school that was several blocks from mine. He never cut classes, but he never told Mom and Dad when I did either. Before my school got out, he'd already be dismissed. Jon had a good idea of where I'd be on a spring day like this one. I knew he just wanted to make sure I was all right and didn't get caught.

"Ready to go?" Jon asked. "Your school's almost out. Better get to Grandma Dorie's at the normal time."

"We were on our way before you ate it," I laughed.

"Shut up, and let's go," he said.

Jon's bike now leaned next to mine and Matthew's. The three of us jumped on our bicycles and rode to my Grandma Dorie and Grandpa Harp's house.

My mother's parents lived only four blocks from my house. Their house was on my way home from school, so I usually stopped there first. Grandma always had something baking or candy to snack on.

The door was propped open with a potted plant, and the three of us charged inside. It was just after three o' clock, and over my shoulder I saw the first group of grade school classmates walking home from school. *Not bad*, I thought.

"Grandma Dorie," I called out, "got anything good?"

"I baked this morning," she answered.

Grandma Dorie was one of those proper ladies from the 1950s. She spent all day cooking, but always dressed nicely, and fixed her hair and make-up first thing in the morning. She believed a lady should look presentable whether she was in the kitchen or going to church. Although Grandma had good manners, she wasn't the type to correct grammar or make us finish our vegetables.

"I hid them from your grandfather," she said. "Jar's in the cupboard."

I grabbed a chocolate chip cookie and passed the jar to Jon and Matthew.

The three of us sat on the front porch as Matthew and I gloated, watching all the kids walking home after finishing their last class. We believed we'd made a clean getaway from school. We were wrong.

At that moment, my family's gray Arrowstar minivan pulled into the driveway, and Mom stepped out, glaring at me.

"Jason, get over here now!" Mom yelled.

When standing back to back, Mom and I were nearly the same height. She had dark, curly hair, cut very short, and on this day she wore a blue baseball cap. From a distance she didn't look all that different from the kids walking home from school. Unlike Grandma Dorie, Mom wasn't concerned with baking or being proper. She was more of a tomboy and could be kind of a bully. Despite her less-than-intimidating size, her wrath was frightening. I was sure to be grounded.

Walking down the black asphalt driveway in the direction of my mother, head drooping, I kicked a rock lying at my feet. With each step I was coming to terms with the fact that I'd be stuck in my room for the next few days.

"Mom, I—" I had my excuses all ready to go, but she cut me off.

"Save it," she growled. "We're late. I'll deal with you playing hooky when we get home."

"Home from where, Mom?"

"You have an appointment with an orthopedist," she said.

"A what?"

"A doctor's appointment."

"No kiddin'," I replied, looking at Matthew and weighing the irony.

A bounce returned to my step and a smile to my face, as new hope of getting away with something filled my thoughts. I'd never been to a doctor's appointment I'd call fun, but an appointment was better than being punished, for sure.

Chapter Two

Small Surgery Called a Biopsy

The bump on my shoulder was a mystery to everyone who examined it. The size, color, and shape of the bump changed slightly at different hours of the day. One thing that didn't change was the fact that if you touched it—it hurt—a lot. I pointed this out to everyone who examined my shoulder, but my words were lost on any person with a medical degree.

"Can I take a look at that?" takes on a whole new meaning coming from the mouth of a doctor.

When a medical examiner of any kind says, "Can I take a look at that?" what he or she means is, "Can I push, yank, and squeeze your shoulder until you scream?"

Then the doctor, resident, or nurse asks, "Does this hurt?"

My parents talked with a number of doctors and I had a series of medical tests. Pokes, pushes, MRI machines, bone scans, and CT scans riddled my life day after day. My parents had been told the bump could be a number of things: a calcium deposit, a cyst or a bone infection. The examinations gave no specific answers, but none of the doctors mentioned anything serious. Nevertheless, because my parents were given no absolute explanation as to what was wrong with me, each physical poke to my skin and shoulder seemed to make them worry more.

Sure, examinations bothered me, but I gave none of them more than an annoyed thought. In the past, every other scratch or scrape, stitch, or cast had healed over time—why should this bump be any different? My job was to be a kid, and I didn't ask questions or pay attention to test results. I left it up to the doctors and my parents to make decisions and worry. For me, each appointment was just an inconvenience of an hour or two.

The doctors' names, faces, and the news they gave faded almost as quickly as the sting from a needle or an inquisitive push on my shoulder. All examinations were a hassle—a blur that I paid little attention to. The nurses and the machines they used to scan my body looked the same as a dozen others I'd seen the day before. Through all of the tests and doctor visits, I carried out my normal and sometimes misguided routine, a routine that on this particular day had led to me cutting school with Matthew.

When my parents and I arrived at the latest doctor's appointment, this time with an orthopedist, my name was soon called by a receptionist. I walked down a similar hall, and into an examining room. Sitting on an examining table identical to a dozen others where I'd sat, a nurse took my blood pressure exactly as a dozen others had done over the past weeks. I took off my shirt and waited in the uncomfortably air-conditioned room for a doctor to push, yank, and squeeze the bump on my shoulder.

This particular doctor was slightly different from the line-up of doctors I'd seen over the past weeks. Dr. Susa lived in our neighborhood and had kids around my age.

"Hello, neighbors," he said when he came in.

"Nice to see you, Dr. Susa," Dad replied.

His white lab coat was the same as other doctors, but under his coat I saw a bright Hawaiian print shirt. Dr. Susa had a big mustache that fluttered when he spoke, reminding me of mud flaps on the back of an eighteen-wheeler truck. His personality was also big and his voice carried. He joked with me while pushing and squeezing the bump on my shoulder. It hurt, but I didn't pay much attention to him. I looked out the window and daydreamed. My mind was distracted with what I'd done before the appointment and what I planned to do after. But, what he had to say next caught my attention.

"Jason needs to have a small surgery," he told my parents, "I'll schedule a biopsy for Monday morning so we can find out what this bump is exactly."

Dr. Susa explained the "pre-op" process, that the surgery would be "outpatient" and would actually be pretty quick. He simply wanted to take out a small piece of the bump and get it analyzed. When he was done talking, the doctor opened the door and escorted my parents and me to the waiting room.

"Everything will be fine," he told Mom and Dad.

From there, we drove to my Grandma Dorie and Grandpa Harp's house. Our entire extended family gathered at Grandma's and Grandpa's almost weekly for birthday parties or family dinners. My grandparents, aunts, uncles, and cousins would be concerned, anxious to learn the latest news about the bump on my shoulder.

Inside, Mom and Dad explained that a biopsy would be performed at six o'clock on Monday morning to find out what exactly was growing on my collarbone.

"At least I don't have to go to school next week," I added.

The mood during dinner was far from sad. We joined hands, Dad said a short prayer, and then the table was filled with food, bottles of wine, laughing aloud, and off-color jokes.

Following dinner, with emotions drained and stomachs full, Mom, Dad, my brother and I walked to our van for the short drive home. My mind was worn by the repetition of the drive. I knew the sight of each block before the houses, fences, and trees were in view. I knew the feel of Dad turning each corner before I was pushed to the right or left of my seat, and the familiar sounds of our gravel driveway crackled under the minivan's tires.

The moon and lamppost in my front yard outlined our house's simple square frame. The lamppost was a little crooked, tilted off plumb, but its light still showed perfectly the cement walkway leading to our front door. With a jingle from Dad's

Small Surgery Called a Biopsy

keys, our front door opened, allowing the sound and scent from our wood fireplace to emerge, revealing the familiar living room, kitchen, hallway, and bedrooms. These spaces lay waiting for my family and me to act out our bedtime routines.

Mom and Dad would walk down the hallway to their room or to the bathroom. My brother Jon would straightaway descend to the basement. I'd make way to my perch at our kitchen counter to drink a glass of milk before bed. The drive, our home, and our routines were familiar and regular. They combated the day's events, which presented uncertainty and the threat of change.

While Mom and Dad brushed their teeth and talked, and my brother was in his room reading, I settled alone in the dimmed kitchen, lit only by the light streaming in from the hallway. I sat, sipped, and thought.

My stomach turned with nervousness when I thought of the biopsy. It was like those first minutes of a basketball game or before a science exam at school. Whenever the biopsy came to mind, I thought about Dr. Susa's assurance: "Everything is going to be fine." Or I'd think of the familiarity of my home, sip my milk, while slowly a sense of calm began to replace my nervousness.

I finished my milk, walked down our hall to my room, and climbed into bed. It was only moments before my mother and father crossed the hallway that separated our rooms and opened my door. Mom tucked me in.

"Brush your teeth?" she asked.

"Got 'em, even the back ones."

She kept looking at me like moms do when they know you're full of it.

"Yeah, I forgot, Mom."

"We'll let it slide this time," she said.

"What a relief. I'll brush extra in the morning."

"The doctor does these little surgeries all the time." Mom changed the subject. "You'll be good as new, Jase."

"I know, Mom."

"Love you," she said.

"Love you, too, Mom."

She gently kissed my forehead and left the room.

Dad turned off the florescent light overhead, and turned the two-click lamp next to my bed only once. He left enough light in the room to allow his eyes to focus on the scripture he had chosen for the evening. His nightly readings to Jon and me usually came from the New Testament. And Dad always sat in a chair he placed next to our beds. When Dad finished reading, he turned off the lamp.

"Jason, I bet a dollar you can't count to ten once they give you the anesthetic," he said calmly.

My father was an even-keeled, deep-thinking sort of guy, with the peaceful nature you'd expect from a pastor. Although Dad had never officiated a marriage without needing to pause the ceremony to wipe tears from his eyes, Mom was the more emotional parent, Dad could generally be counted on to calm things down.

"How about twenty bucks?" I said, looking up at him hopefully. My dad was stocky with a thick, dark beard, and hands that were rough from fishing in Alaska or fixing things around our house. He often smoked a pipe or Backwoods cigars while he was working outside or in our garage.

Dad finally agreed to the twenty bucks. The sweet smell of tobacco clung to his beard, fingertips, and flannel shirt as he shook my hand firmly and pulled me close.

"Deal," he whispered.

"Deal," I repeated.

* * * * *

A Look Back: My Family and Me

My parents met at a college football game in Bozeman, Montana, where my father grew up, and where he and my mother attended Montana State University. Even then they were "holy-rollers," or, looking at the pictures, Christian hippies might be a better description.

My father wore bellbottomed jeans with a cross embroidered into the pocket. My mother carried a classical guitar with the letters P.T.L. (Praise the Lord) painted on it, which she received as a gift after being baptized in the Clark Fork River. As the story goes, my father noticed her leaving the football game and said confidently to a friend, "I'm going to marry that girl."

They dated for less than a month when Dad proposed marriage. When he told his parents and my mother's parents that he was going to propose, they all reacted very differently. Grandpa Greer was calm and looked over his newspaper as he solemnly addressed his son, "If you break that little girl's heart, you are going to be in big trouble." Everyone knew my grandfather on my mother's side as Harp, a shortened version of the last name "Harper." To us grandkids, he was Grandpa Harp; to everyone else he was just Harp. When my father addressed him by Frank, his actual first name, Grandpa knew it was to say something important. When Dad asked his permission to marry my mother, Harp was ecstatic. He jumped up out of his chair and hugged his soon-to-be son-in-law. Then Grandpa Harp went to the liquor store and bought an entire case of Scotch whiskey to celebrate.

My parents were married in Missoula in 1976. About a year after their wedding, my mother became pregnant with Jon. Her pregnancy with my older brother was without incident, and in 1977, Jon was born; he was a gorgeous and good-tempered baby. As a result of Jon's good nature, I was conceived a little over a year later.

While I was still in the womb, I kicked my mother so hard that I broke some of her ribs. Following several long hours of labor, I was born with a crooked nose, scowling at the doctor. My father said I looked like a boxer who had just lost a title fight. As an infant I was neither gorgeous nor good-tempered. I screamed and hollered, and Jon sometimes patted my mother's stomach and begged, "Please put Jason back, Mommy. He wasn't done cookin' yet."

Returning to the womb was, of course, not an option. But in the first months of life, my parents promised each other to never have another child.

Still, there had rarely been an occasion when it was just my mother, father, Jon, and me living in our house. Throughout my childhood, dozens of extra people lived in our home. Although, "There were always people coming and going," as Tom Hanks said in Forrest Gump, our house did not look like a Southern plantation. It was small, a bright red rambler with five little bedrooms. The rooms were almost always filled. I even recall a bed being set up in the storage closet, and the washer and dryer sitting in a downstairs hallway because someone was living in the laundry room. The various tenants were people passing through, connected to my family by our church, foster kids lost in the juvenile system, and university students who volunteered for non-profit organizations in the area. Renters paid what they were able to, but as long as there was space in our house, my parents turned no one away.

Small Surgery Called a Biopsy

It was not just a lively house or the grandeur of the area that made Missoula a memorable hometown. It is the home of a liberal arts university, downtown Missoula has many historic buildings and a few streets are still paved with red brick. East and westbound trains bring transients to Missoula every spring and summer, adding eccentric folk singers, and hobos who smelled like stale beer dwell in the entryways of the old downtown buildings. The city had well over thirty thousand residents by the time I was born. Nevertheless, as a boy I felt like it was a tiny town. It was a place where people knew you by your first name, enjoyed the Saturday morning Farmers' Markets, and remained largely unaffected by serious crime. Neither Missoula nor my family was perfect, but I have fond memories of growing up there.

Things were relatively quiet at our little house in the spring of 1991. Just before discovering I had cancer, only my parents, Jon, and I officially lived in our home. Having a small bump on my shoulder but no idea just how our lives would be turned upside-down by its appearance, the four of us and a group of high school students traveled to an orphanage in a poor part of Mexico.

I don't know exactly why this trip became so relevant to fighting cancer. Perhaps it was the stories I had heard from my parents or those passing through our house. Witnessing difficulty, even atrocities, observing the strength of the human spirit and personal faith were no longer just tales told at a Bible study after a spaghetti dinner. I was there. The streets outside of this orphanage were rough and scarred, as were the men and women who walked them. But inside its walls dwelt something peculiar. The cast-iron gate separating the entrance of the orphanage from the rest of the world was a step into safety. As the children walked through these gates, instantaneously, the scowls they needed to survive in the harsh reality of the outside world were erased, and replaced with grins.

For the first time I witnessed a happiness that was in no way based on material possessions or the "American Dream." Brick walls took the place of white picket fences. Razor-sharp fragments of glass were cemented and fastened to the top of the walls finishing their construction. A halo of barbed wire hung above the walls, casting shadows upon the cemented broken glass. The glass and the circle of barbed wire were not there to keep the children in, but to protect them from the world outside of the orphanage—the walls provided a place of safety.

Seeing joy on the faces of children who appeared to have nothing would eventually lead me to the conclusion that they must have something special. This joy was the result of a gift. That gift did not come in the form of toys or clothes, but it was wrapped around them, and would prove to be something so much more than an object occupying space in a toy box. The people who passed through the brick walls and came into contact with these children could not help but give their hearts away, genuinely caring for others without expectation. To see smiles replace the tears, and a feeling of safety replace the fear as a result of people simply being selfless proved to be a stirring reward.

* * * * *

I woke up from surgery in sudden pain. It seemed like only a few minutes after I had arrived in the operating room for the biopsy that consciousness crashed against me. At first, nausea and an aching body overwhelmed me, as the pain and sickness lessened, I drifted back to sleep. The pattern repeated itself. Ankle-deep in consciousness, I swayed between awake and asleep—each time unable to stay awake—each time unable to remain asleep.

Pain in my shoulder and nausea in my stomach kept me from really resting, and the anesthetic and total exhaustion kept me from fully waking up. I couldn't get past the grogginess from the medications I had been given throughout and following the biopsy. For almost two days, my eyes never opened up all the way.

Each passing hour left me less groggy, and every time I woke up I tried to sharpen all the thoughts the drugs had dulled. I tried to figure out which were dreams and what was actually real; I could only figure out a couple of things. First, I understood that my surgery hadn't been an "outpatient" procedure after all; I was in a real hospital room. And that room was full of my friends and relatives from near and far away.

Though my eyes weren't open, I heard and recognized voices. Grandma and Grandpa Greer, Grandma Dorie and Grandpa Harp, my Uncle Greg, my brother Jon, my cousins, and some close friends filled my room. A room filled to the brim with voices was nothing out of the ordinary for my family. But these voices were filled with quivers and pauses. I heard sniffles and broken sentences all around me—a deep sense of sadness surrounded my hospital bed.

As I listened closely, I gathered my wits about me and forced the dreams away, wandering through the reasons why my family would be crying. Straining to hear, the sniffles and unfinished words were less noticeable. Distinct sobs were scattered throughout the room. The deepest and loudest were the sobs let out by Mom, sitting next to my hospital bed. *Am I dreaming? Why would my family be crying?* I was confused, nauseous, and my shoulder ached.

In frustration, I asked, "Mom, why're you crying?"

Hush draped each corner of the room, muting out the sounds of sniffles, shaky whispers, crinkling tissues, and sobbing. A few long seconds passed and the silence frightened me.

"It's because you're so pale, Jason," she replied.

I hardly ever questioned Mom. Plus, her answer was exactly what I wanted to hear. It calmed me down, satisfied my questions, and put me at ease. Forgetting about the tears and the sobs, I fell back to sleep and didn't sway in or out until waking to all my wits the next morning.

Chapter Three

Bicycles, Baseball Cards, Oncology, and Chemotherapy

The hospital room had emptied, and only Mom and Dad stood by my bed. I felt good enough to sit up and talk to my parents. Seeing color return to my face, Mom called a doctor.

"Jason looks like he's recovering," she said into the phone. "Could you come up and check on him?"

A few hours passed before two doctors stood at the door. One was Dr. Susa, who was both our neighbor and the man who had operated on me. I didn't recognize the other man. He wasn't a part of the string of doctors I'd seen so far. He wore a short-sleeved silk dress shirt and glasses with lenses that were perfectly round.

"How're you?" Dr. Susa asked.

"Pretty good."

"Good." Dr. Susa said, looking at the man with perfectly round glasses. "Jason, this is Dr. Speckart. He's an oncologist here in Missoula."

Out of the corner of my eye, I saw Mom wince at the word *oncologist*. Whatever that meant, it wasn't good.

The new doctor walked in and sat at the foot of my hospital bed. The top of his head was bald and suntanned. Whatever hair that was left was dark brown, uncut, and tightly curled, making him look like an absent-minded professor kind of genius—the kind who just might be able to answer any question I asked him.

"Nice to meet you, Jason," Dr. Speckart said, patting my leg.

"Nice to meet you, Mister," I replied.

Dad put his arm around Mom, and I could see that his jaw was clinched. The two of them were listening closely, kind of leaning in to whatever Dr. Speckart had to say.

The change in my parents signaled for me to pay close attention, too. I didn't look out the window or imagine the many places I'd rather be. I focused, waiting, ready to listen.

"Have you talked to your parents about the surgery?" the doctor asked politely, but I could tell he was serious.

"Not really," I replied.

Dr. Speckart looked at me and swallowed, "Jason, you have Ewing's Sarcoma."

His voice was sure—pointed. There didn't seem to be any reason for me to think that what I had was scary, but the hairs on my neck still rose.

Suddenly, my voice didn't sound like me.

"Is...is...there a cure for Ewing...Sarcoma?" I stuttered.

Another four-cornered silence followed my question. I'd sat next to my grade school principal enough to recognize seriousness in a conversation. I knew something was wrong. The silence following my question turned anxiety into anger.

My eyes locked onto Dr. Speckart, insisting he respond; he answered with an almost surprising, "Yes."

Yes, there's a cure, so what's the problem? What's everyone worried about?

"What's the cure?" I asked.

My parents flinched when the doctor said "chemotherapy." This was the first time I'd heard this vocabulary word. To me, chemotherapy was just one more big name. I was simply glad to know there was a cure.

My conversation with Dr. Speckart continued, and it was comfortable. The funny thing was, while we talked, both of my parents started crying. They weren't blubbering or anything, but tears were running down Mom's and Dad's faces, pretty steadily. Dad had his arm around Mom, holding her tightly. He wiped his wet cheeks every few minutes. Every so often, he'd go pull a fresh tissue from a box on the windowsill and hand it to Mom. I didn't understand what was wrong with them.

Why're Mom and Dad freaking out?

Dr. Speckart threw around some other big words, but they meant nothing to me. The doctor told me he was an oncologist and I told him I was a football player. He told me about chemotherapy and I told him about my baseball cards. He told me about malignancy and I told him about my bike. I was told I had some disease, with some weird name, and that there was some sort of cure for whatever I had. "Chemotherapy" and "cure" were the facts I was given after the biopsy. I was going to be fine.

Probably a million facts about Ewing's Sarcoma and chemotherapy were left out that morning, and probably for good reason. But I was told that our family would be taking a long trip. An hour or two after my surgery, long before I woke up from the anesthetic, my parents had already made a decision to leave Missoula. After talking with the two doctors, Mom and Dad decided we'd be traveling to Seattle, Washington, to the Children's Hospital.

"The bump on your shoulder was removed," Dr. Susa said, "and I even scraped the bone to get rid of the tumor. But for the best treatment, you'll need to leave home for a while."

"How long'll we be gone?" I asked.

Dr. Susa looked at Dr. Speckart. "Doctor?" he asked, passing on my question.

"Well, it will be up to the doctors in Seattle, Jason. But you should be prepared for at least three or four months."

Bicycles, Baseball Cards, Oncology, and Chemotherapy

Dr. Speckart made sure I had no more questions before he politely excused himself from the room. Dr. Susa stayed a while longer. He talked with Mom and Dad, offering them encouragement about the Children's Hospital in Seattle.

"If it were my kid, I'd be going to Children's," he told them. "I did my residency under Dr. Chappie Conrad. He's the best."

"Good luck, Jase," Dr. Susa's eyes began to fill, and he choked on the words. I could tell that he wasn't going to be able to finish his sentence. In a rush, he left the room.

Dad followed Dr. Susa out into the hall. A few minutes later, he was back, quietly filling in my Mom on what happened.

"He was out there leaning against the wall. He looked like he was going to collapse," I heard Dad say.

"Is he okay?" Mom wanted to know.

"Yeah." Dad sighed. "I asked him, 'How many times in a doctor's career do you think he's gotta tell a kid he has bone cancer?'"

"What did Dr. Susa say?"

"God willing…only once."

"And then…" Mom quizzed.

"And then I told him, 'Good news. You're done.'"

* * * * *

A Look Back: Cancer

Something had gone wrong among the smallest parts of me. The pattern in chemical material inherited from my parents had changed. My DNA was damaged beyond repair. DNA is responsible for all cell activities. It guides normal cells in an orderly manner as they grow, divide, and then die. Some of my cells did not behave as normal cells. They outlasted regular, orderly cells, and in turn each abnormal cell formed additional abnormal cells—two became four, four became eight, and eight became sixteen. Inside my body, cancer cells multiplied out of control.

In the case of Ewing's Sarcoma, my specific type of bone cancer, DNA was damaged somewhere between chromosome 11 and chromosome 22. Cells reproduced and gathered into a solid tumor that had attached to my collarbone. If nothing was done to stop the abnormal cells from multiplying, cancerous tumors would grow in size and number all over my body. Eventually they would fill my lungs, attach to my bones, heart, or head, greedily pushing from the inside out, leaving no room for life.

The problem of damaged DNA and abnormal cells was not inherited from my parents. The change in my body had happened after my birth; my disease was not contagious and could not be blamed on radiation, chemicals, or any other environmental factor. The cause remains unknown. There was no finger of blame to be pointed and there was no substitute or person to take my place. Although it seems I was too young, I had to stand amid this storm and fight to get through it myself.

The fight was mine to endure, but clenched in my fists was the knowledge and progress of generations. Doctors and scientists had spent their lives combating cancer; lifetimes of dedication to the medical field had built one on top of the other, and over centuries ideas multiplied—two became four, four became eight, and eight became sixteen. *Discoveries made by strangers that I could only know in books shone light on this unpredictable disease and gave me the medical advancements that allowed me to fight cancer.*

During my personal fight with cancer I was surrounded by the historic signatures of those who had answered the call, "What say you?" The ancient Greek physician Hippocrates, who is considered the father of medicine, is credited with clearly defining the difference between benign and malignant tumors. Hippocrates observed that the blood around malignant tumors (like the one on my collarbone) resembled a crab's claw. The disease became known as karkinoma, the Greek word for crab. Eventually the Latin word for crab, cancer, replaced the preceding term.

The study of medicine furthered and was nurtured by Galileo and Newton in their respective developments of the scientific method. Giovanni Morgagni of Padua performed autopsies relating a patient's illness to the pathologic findings after death. In doing so he laid the groundwork for the study of cancer: oncology. In the life of Morgagni, the famous surgeon Jon Hunter believed that some cancers could be cured by surgery. In 1846, fifty-three years after Hunter's death, anesthesia became available. Anesthesia so rapidly advanced surgical operations that the next hundred years became known as "the century of the surgeon." In the 1920s, Dr. James Ewing first observed and defined the characteristics of a solid tumor that commonly attached to the pelvis, thigh, lower leg, upper arm, and rib, and the cancer was named Ewing's Sarcoma.

Nearing the end of the century of the surgeon, a fortuitous discovery was made which began the use of chemotherapy. In 1956, the first metastatic cancer was successfully treated with the use of methotrexate, a chemotherapy drug that remains in use today.

I was not treated with methotrexate, but my treatment included similar drugs that came about because of its success. Discoveries over time, especially in the 1970s and 1980s, gave me a chance to fight and survive. The chemotherapy drugs that I was given were still being used fifteen years later. The potency of the drugs and the number of months in which they were administered had decreased, lessening the side effects from the poison.

Through the best oncologists, surgeons, nurses, technicians, and researchers of my time, I was able to take advantage of the advances in modern medicine. Advances have progressed since my diagnosis, protocol, and remission. Because of constant medical discovery, I was more fortunate than a child treated for cancer in the years before my diagnosis, just as it is more fortunate to be diagnosed this year than in 1991. More children live through cancer today than ever before, but it remains a dangerous disease.

Even by today's standards I am fortunate to have my life.

* * * * *

One night not long before we left for Seattle, I stayed over at Grandma Dorie and Grandpa Harp's house. This was pretty normal for me. I had a bedroom there, too, and I spent almost as much time growing up at Grandma's as I did at home. I guess it was the lengthy four-block walk back to my house that forced me to sleep over so frequently. Well, I suppose it also could've been the cable television, cookies, and soda pop. Mom's only recipe was written on the back of a mac-and-cheese box, and the TV often didn't work at my house.

I sat at the counter in my grandparents' kitchen with my Uncle Greg. Everyone else was in bed. Except for the two of us, the house and the neighborhood looked abandoned. It was like many other evenings we'd spent at the kitchen counter.

Bicycles, Baseball Cards, Oncology, and Chemotherapy

Uncle Greg was a college student at the University in Missoula. He was my mother's younger brother, but wasn't much like Mom. Other than both having dark, curly hair, they didn't look alike, and he slept in on Sundays instead of going to church. He was more like an older brother to me and Jon than an uncle. He taught us about poker, the line of scrimmage and how to spit.

I liked it when Uncle Greg joined me and my friends for after-school games of street football and home-run derby. He'd be the umpire or an all-time quarterback. He was there the day when we were playing football, at that moment when the bump on my shoulder was hit and I fell down in tears. I didn't cry very often, so Greg knew something was wrong. He's the one who made me tell Mom right away.

So much had happened since then. On this quiet night, we sat at the counter and talked and talked, but not about cards or the line of scrimmage. My uncle and I talked about the changes in my life. We talked about chemotherapy, and how I couldn't wait for the fall to come so I could play on my football team again.

"Can't wait to get the next couple of months over with," I said cheerfully. "Do chemotherapy real quick this spring. Then, good as new, and football in fall."

I didn't really know what chemotherapy was, what I'd be exposed to, or how to make a cup of soup on my own for that matter. My world was small and sheltered.

"You'll be fine, Jase, but cancer is a tough one," Uncle Greg said. "You might want to take a season off. Play next year when you're all healed up. Wait until you're a hundred percent and can get a TD every game."

The light both inside and outside of the house was faint. Greg and I sat in a dimly lit kitchen, which sat in a dimly lit town, but slowly my situation was becoming clearer. Greg was the first person to say the word "cancer" to me. Until then, everybody said I had Ewing's Sarcoma, a weird name with only one word attached to its definition: *Yes*.

"Yes," there was a cure. "Yes," I'd be fine, and "Yes," life would return to normal. Much more was attached to the word *cancer*, even for an eleven-year-old kid like me.

I'd never personally known anyone with cancer. But I'd overheard grown-ups talking about people with cancer. "So and so, who was a friend of a friend, who had cancer and was sick." I didn't know what cancer really was or how it worked, but the images that "cancer" brought up were frightening. Shaken by the new word attached to me, I fired question after question at Uncle Greg. Greg wasn't a doctor or anything; he only knew a few answers, but that was more than I knew.

"How long'll chemotherapy take?" I asked, and without waiting, launched into more questions. "Will it take long to recover? A week? Month, maybe? Maybe I should wait a year to play football, really hit the weights, go jogging and stuff, like *Rocky IV*. What do you think?"

"Don't know, buddy," Uncle Greg answered. "I think those are all questions for when you get to Seattle. They have the best doctors there. They'll tell you all about your cancer and chemotherapy."

Uncle Greg took a moment to think, and then began, "To make you better...they have to give you like a poison that'll kill the cells in your body. That's the chemo. It kills the cancer cells, but some of the good cells, too."

"Will chemo hurt?" I asked.

"Yes," he answered.

"What kind of hurt?" I kept on.

"Well, it might make you sick, like having the flu, mostly," he said. "And one other thing…"

"What?"

"You could lose your hair."

"Seriously?"

"Yeah, but it'll grow back." Uncle Greg filled me in on what he knew, the stereotypes, the basics of an awful disease, and a cure that sounded even worse.

"How do you know all of this? Did you know someone with cancer?" I asked.

"No. I think everybody knows a little, buddy," he answered.

I'd seen some real problems on TV or when Mom and Dad talked about the headlines. But there had always been a separation between me and those news stories, the children at an orphanage in Mexico, or foster kids who moved in to our home. Before now, the only scares really facing my life were making the basketball team, getting detention or walking home from school in winter. All of a sudden, bubblegum and skinned knees seemed like they were kind of behind me. In front of me were chemotherapy and IVs.

Speaking with Greg and thinking back on medical exams, my biopsy, Ewing's Sarcoma, and cancer, my life seemed colder, grayer, broken and in need of fixing when compared to growing up pretty much worry-free. For the first time, I glimpsed a threat in my own life: a trouble growing closer.

Chapter Four

Send Off

Springtime didn't care that I had cancer. The morning shined as April mornings had year after year. My neighborhood burst with the heroes of a normal Montana spring: blue sky and dandelions, rain from the night before sitting on blades of grass, and warm sun that caused the yellow flowers and grass to look polished and brand new.

I sat on the front steps of my house, resting my chin in the palm of my right hand. My arm pressed against my knee, comfortably holding up my hand and head. My left arm was also cradled. A dark blue sling strapped tightly against my body held it absolutely still to help my shoulder heal from the biopsy. I sat, head in hand, and watched the sun and flowers, grass and sky play their part in a favorite time of year; they were sure of their place and role in the morning and season.

Family, friends, neighbors, and other people I didn't recognize, people unsure of their role in this morning, also passed by me. They were extra careful when walking past me, patting my back delicately, not certain how breakable I really was—some saying nothing, others asking repeatedly if I needed anything.

"All packed," I replied.

A swarm of people moved from the front door of our house to the driveway, where our minivan and Harp's motor home were parked. Dozens of people helped my family load up our things. I think everything we owned was packed in either our van or the motor home. I imagined us driving away on summer vacation with the motor home's destination Yellowstone Park or Disneyland—but no. Grandma Dorie, Grandpa Harp, Mom and Dad, Jon, and I, we were all going to Seattle on a different kind of trip.

Starting the very day I was diagnosed with cancer, it seemed like everybody in Missoula wanted to help our family. Women from Mom's Bible study brought us bags of groceries, casseroles, and a chicken pot pie. Others from the church sent dozens of "Get well" cards. One person even gave my parents quite a collection of miniature shampoo bottles—a lifetime supply, I think. Not long ago, my grade school held a bake sale and live auction that raised money to help with medical bills. I was too sick to go, but Grandpa Harp bid on the biggest, brightest, orangiest cowboy hat I'd ever seen, and brought it home to me.

Someone probably put that big, orange cowboy hat in the motor home, I thought.

It was late in the day when the minivan and motor home were finally packed and we were ready to leave Missoula. People had run out of work to do. A few still buzzed around looking for some last-minute way to help Mom and Dad, but most hung out on our front yard, just waiting to say good-bye. By the time I stood up and began walking to the motor home, most of the lawn was filled with friends and family.

I walked through the crowd, hugging people and shaking hands while they said things like, "Go get 'em," "Keep your chin up," and "We'll be praying." Some smiled and others cried. I went through the line as fast as I could—I hated long good-byes. When I reached the steps of the motor home, I turned and took a hard look behind me before going inside.

I saw my friends from school who'd go on fishing and hunting, climbing trees, and impatiently waiting for summer. I saw family who'd return to work. When we pulled out of the drive, all of these kids and grown-ups would go back to their everyday lives, in our town, in this Montana spring.

Looking past the faces, I studied our small part of Montana. Two streets intersected, making up my family's address. I looked at the old wooden fence following the corner exactly, bending with the curb as one street turned into the other. The splintered fence bordered our front yard, which was always overdue for mowing. The bushy grass was tall and I don't think anything could have been greener that day. Our lawn made the fire-engine-red house where I'd lived my whole life pop out like a picture book. I tried to etch it all into my thoughts. I never wanted to dig deep for the memory of home. I looked forward to the day when I could come back here, when I could blend in again, when changes would be normal again, like the seasons.

I opened the motor home's door and stepped up. We were packed and it was time to go, but that didn't mean we'd be driving away just yet. I knew I'd be the first person ready to leave and that Mom would be the last. I couldn't rush her, no doubt about that, so I planned on finding a comfy spot to sit and wait. I thought I'd be alone, but inside the motor home I found good company.

Uncle Greg and Grandpa Greer were sitting on the couch, each planning to give me a present and say good-bye quietly away from the crowd.

Greg had two gifts. Neither one was wrapped. A blanket was on his lap, and a small book was in his left hand. He handed me the blanket first and I opened it up. It was a quilt with a gigantic black-and-white soccer ball stitched on the front.

"To remind you of home when you're going to sleep," he said.

Once again, Greg neatly folded the blanket. Then, he handed me the small book. It was a leather-bound journal. I opened it and was flipping through the pages when I discovered that he'd made the first entry himself.

"*April 13, 1991*

"*I just wanted everyone to know that my Uncle Greg is the best-looking guy in the world, and he knows everything about everything—signed Jason.*"

I smiled up at him. "Thanks, Uncle Greg."

Careful of my shoulder, he hugged me around the sling and, without another word, turned and left.

It was just Grandpa Greer and me now, and we sat together on the couch. Grand-

Send Off

pa Greer was tall and soft-spoken. He walked and talked very much like my dad, but Grandpa was a little lankier. He always seemed to be humming the tune to one church hymn or another. Grandpa Greer also had a gift. He pulled a small box out of his pocket and handed it to me. Inside was a small ring.

It was silver and smooth and fit perfectly around my pinky. The ring's shape was the same all around, except for the places where two arches pushed out of opposite sides, creating the emblem of a fish. I knew my grandfather made jewelry in his spare time, and I'd seen the emblem before. But I had no idea what the fish meant or why Grandpa had made it for me. I guess he knew I was confused.

"A long, long time ago, people weren't allowed to speak about our faith," he began. "Christians were beaten and killed by Greeks and Romans for having their beliefs. They could be imprisoned…fed to wild animals. It was dangerous to talk about Jesus, so people had to be careful."

"The fish was a symbol used by Greeks and Romans for many years, making it an inconspicuous choice for Christians. A person walking on a road or a beach would make a single arch in the dirt or the sand. If another person had the same faith they'd make an arch in the opposite direction, starting at the tip and crossing at the tail, creating the symbol of a fish. Then, men and women knew they shared the same beliefs, and could talk about their faith and avoid prison or fighting in the Coliseum. The fish became a symbol of martyrs, an emblem of sacrifice."

"They were tested, Jason, but it only made them stronger," my grandfather concluded.

I liked the gift and the story, but was still not sure why he'd made the ring.

"Why did you—?" I was cut short.

The motor home door swung open. Grandpa Harp was standing in the doorway hollering something to Mom, who was simultaneously hollering something back to him. With both voices barreling at the same time, no one could understand what either one of them said. Harp turned and noticed Grandpa Greer and me.

"Hey, guys, you ready to go?" he asked.

"Been ready for a while," I replied.

Grandpa Greer and I stood as Harp walked over to the couch. I gave Grandpa Greer a hug.

"Thanks, Gramps," I said.

Next he turned and hugged Grandpa Harp.

I smiled at the picture of the two men. I'd never heard Grandpa Greer raise his voice, but Grandpa Harp could hoot and holler with the best of them. Grandpa Greer was tall and lanky. Grandpa Harp was short and had a beer belly that hung just below his belt straps. Grandpa Greer always had a black comb sticking from his back pocket, which he used to slick back his straight white hair before dinner. Grandpa Harp didn't have much hair left on his head; the few remaining strands were tightly coiled and stuck straight up no matter how often they were combed. One was a pilot and a scientist, and the other was a sailor and a salesman. One served in the Air Force, the other in the Navy, but both served in the same war. However different, Grandpa Greer and Grandpa Harp each had that all-the-time grandfather smile that didn't even budge for stuff like cancer and chemo.

Grandpa Harp moved to the driver's seat of the motor home and fired up its Ford

460 big-block engine. On top of his head, he placed a mesh-backed baseball cap with the insignia "U.S.S. *Anacostia*." Harp wore his cap loosely so he could tip it to one side or the other and block the sun wherever it shined. With his hat tipped, cockeyed, as if he had one too many martinis, Harp revved the motor home engine loudly to let everyone know that it was time to leave.

Grandpa Greer hummed softly as he moved toward the door. Before he left, he gave me a wink, a last wave and then stepped outside.

The roar of the motor home engine was the sign to get in, or get left behind. In a lull of the engine's gust, Grandpa Harp poked his head from the driver's side window and let out one last family-known warning.

"Clear the prop!" Harp yelled.

My brother and grandmother scrambled up the motor home steps. The call by my grandfather and the engine of the motor home even broke through Mom's long good-byes. She joined Dad, climbing in the front seat of our family's van.

"Here we go," Grandpa Harp said.

PHOTOS
Growing Up – Before Cancer

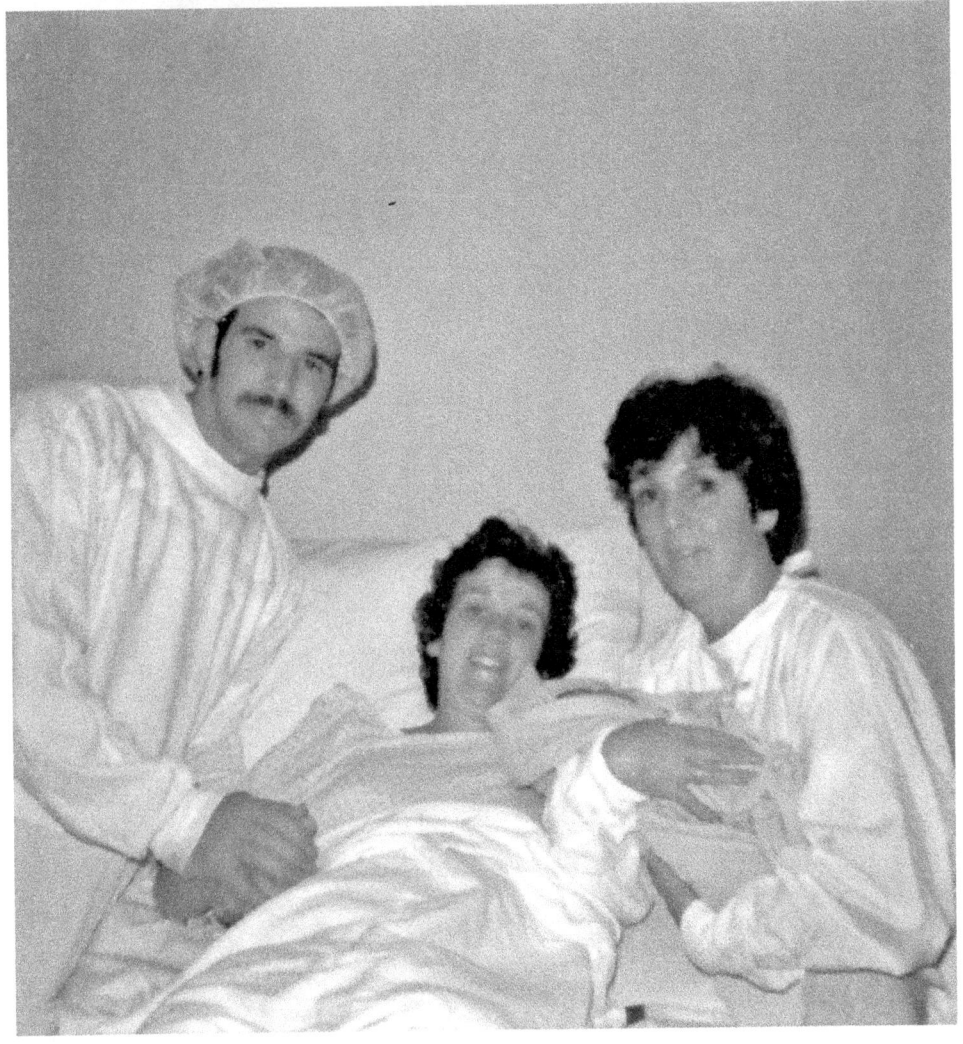

Dad, Mom, Grandma Dorie holding newborn Jason. Missoula, Montana, 1979.

Jon, Jason and their father, Jeff at Grandma and Grandpa Greer's house. Bozeman, Montana, 1981.

Jason and big brother, Jon at a combined birthday celebration. Missoula, Montana, 1982.

Greer family on summer vacation. Going to the Sun Highway, 1984.

Chapter Five

A Thousand Zip Codes from Home

Seattle was louder than Missoula. The buildings were taller and people moved faster. Cars honked at Grandpa Harp, drivers gave him the finger and angrily sped past. My grandfather simply waved at the other motorists. At the wheel of the motor home, he didn't like to speed up or slow down.

"Got to keep her at fifty-five, or it screws up my mileage," he said over and over, as if the passing cars could hear him.

Harp had been driving his motor home for years, and when the topic of his motor home or motor homes in general came up, no one argued with him about what was best—we just agreed. With only an address and a map on the dashboard, he drove us to a place called the "Ronald McDonald House" without making a single wrong turn.

The Ronald McDonald House is a kind of hotel for families facing illnesses like mine. It'd be our home while away from Missoula. My family and I would have a room at the house, and outside in the parking lot, Grandma and Grandpa would have plenty of space and available electricity for the motor home.

We didn't know what the Ronald McDonald House would look like, how many days we'd be staying, or how many other families would be there, too. My family only knew that Dr. Speckart had recommended the place, and that it was especially for families who needed somewhere to stay while having treatment for cancer.

Grandpa Harp pulled into the parking lot. Grandma, Grandpa, Jon, and I glued ourselves to the motor home windows and looked the building over. Jon and I shoved each other, struggling for more space at the window and a better view of the house. Then Jon looked for a long moment at my arm in a sling, and finally gave up.

"Little jerk's gonna get away with everything now," I heard Jon grumble as he walked away.

From the outside, the Ronald McDonald House was inviting and didn't look very different from other away-from-home places where I'd stayed in the past. But when I walked inside, I found myself not only at the doorway of a new home, but the beginning of a different kind of life. I'd be sleeping in a bed a thousand zip codes away from my familiar room in Missoula. And, judging by first impressions, I'd be living with other kids who seemed distanced even further from all my friends at home.

A Ronald McDonald volunteer guided the six of us through the house. Nothing inside the house was familiar, not a kitchen, hallway, front room, or friend. We were told that the house was built to promote interaction between all of the families staying in its rooms. It had a big kitchen for everyone to use, play rooms for young children, video games for teenagers, a library for parents, and a small playground in its backyard. The shared space inside the house made it hard to be alone, and different than anywhere I'd been before.

The tour attached a real place and real faces to the words "chemotherapy" and "cancer." Inside, we saw firsthand, for the first time, the effects cancer has on mothers, fathers, brothers, sisters, and patients. Many of the kids going from the kitchen to the playroom, or the library to the teen room, were bald.

Uncle Greg and I had already discussed my hair falling out. It might surprise you, but I didn't really care about that. A bunch of my sports heroes and some of the men in my family were bald. I knew I'd lose my hair at some point: *forty-five or eleven, who's counting?* But the children at the McDonald House not only had baldheads. Their sickness was obvious and awful—no eyebrows or eyelashes, some were skinny like they hadn't eaten in a year, and others had puffed up faces, strangely swollen like they were holding air in their cheeks.

There was lots of energy at the house. Children played and laughter came from many of its rooms. Even with skipping and running, laughing and singing, I was aware of the sickness all around me, and it made me cringe. The worst part, even more than the skinniness or swollen cheeks, were the dark circles beneath the kids' sunken eyes.

"Hey, you want to come play?" one sick boy was asking.

"You want some of my treats?" asked another bald kid, lifting an open palm full of M&Ms.

"No, thanks," I said, twice, and I walked closer to Dad.

The image of kids fighting cancer stung me. It made all my muscles stiffen and I wanted to pull away from the other people at the house. I didn't look like them. I didn't feel sick. I didn't think I belonged at the Ronald McDonald House.

The tour ended in Room 9, which was where my family and I would stay while we were in Seattle. It looked like a motel room. There were two double beds, a TV, a bathroom, and a rollaway bed. I sat on the rollaway and looked out the window.

My stomach twisted as I thought of the sick children I'd met. The Ronald McDonald House stirred up more questions, and more confusing feelings. *Is cancer making the kids hurt? Chemo? Will they be better soon? Where do I fit in?* I could only wonder.

* * * * *

A Look Back: Brightly Colored, Cold and Gray

I understood Ewing's Sarcoma was a dangerous disease, but I had a limited understanding of its texture, specifics, or details. What would cancer look like? What would chemo feel like? How long would treatment last? I wondered about the changes in my life and my lack of knowledge caused me to associate them with vague, dreary words like "cold" and "gray."

Cancer and chemotherapy were not gifts wrapped in shiny paper that I longed to open. Yet, I desperately wanted all of their characteristics to be revealed. There was an unmistakable desire inside to define this disease and all of its extremities (a feeling similar to nervously peeking through my fingers during the scary scene in a late-night movie). Giving my new circumstances texture and detail was frightening and made my stomach turn. However, seeing them more clearly also placed limits on my fear, which was less scary than facing an immense, cold, powerful, undefined gray.

When we arrived at Children's Hospital and the Ronald McDonald House, I had no indication of what a child fighting this disease would look like. My reaction to the picture of other children fighting cancer was terrifying. It had no elements of anger or disgust, but was laced from bottom to top with wonder.

Wonder flickers in the eyes of a person the first time that they hear the sound of their newborn baby crying or the cracking sound a baseball bat makes the first time a home run is hit. It appears the first time someone sees the ocean or hears "I Have a Dream." Wonder also appears the first time a loved one dies, a country declares war, or a child hears, "You have cancer."

I have come to think of some wonder as brightly colored and some as a cold gray. I have felt the exhilaration of seeing the ocean for the first time and of hitting my first home run. In those moments wonder, like a bright color, pressed firmly against me and the world was warm and inviting. When my discussion with Greg in my grandparent's kitchen helped me understand I had cancer, and when I witnessed the first-hand affects this disease had on other children, I was also filled with wonder. But it was not warm or inviting. It was cold and gray.

Chapter Six

IV Stand, Skateboards, and Prosthetic Leg Sword Fights

    The Children's Hospital looked like some sort of white castle. It had corridors and hallways and maybe even hidden passageways. There was so much hospital to my right and left that I couldn't tell where it ended, and because Children's was built on a hill, the walk up the drive made an already big hospital look even bigger. I stared up at the large collection of walls and windows curling over and around the green hillside. With each step forward I appeared to be shrinking, and with each step forward the building appeared to grow. Although the hospital was colossal and I felt puny standing next to it, Mom, Dad, and I had to storm the place because everything we needed to get back home again was somewhere inside. But finding the right tests, offices, and doctors turned out to be much more confusing than I'd hoped.
    Dad told me buildings had been added as Children's grew, and the additions were connected to each other by indoor walkways stretching all over the hillside. Some of the buildings started on top of the hill, others had a first floor closer to the hill's bottom. Different floors didn't always match up with the numbers assigned to them. You could travel to the fourth floor, never go up a staircase or take an elevator, and somehow find yourself on the seventh floor. Likewise, you could push the "4" button in an elevator, get off, wander around for a while wondering why every sign read, "6th Floor." The one thing that was the same—the white halls, tile, walls, and doors: they were all identical.
    My parents and I wandered and fumbled and asked directions. We were lost and found and then were lost again. We zigzagged to bone scans and CT scans, blood tests and X-rays. We passed toddlers and teenagers, children in wheelchairs and on crutches. I noticed girls who tried to hide their bald heads with long wigs and boys

in baseball caps who did the same. We also passed other children who were simply at the hospital getting stitches for a cut chin or finger.

It was late afternoon when we got to the room for our last appointment: the "Bone Tumor Clinic." All of the important medical decisions were going to happen here.

We entered a bright room and I found a seat while Mom and Dad checked in with the receptionist. The waiting room had blue and red walls, which made it inviting, different from the white halls we'd been wandering.

Toys and games were stacked around the edges of the room, and there was a gigantic tank filled with tropical fish in the center. Little kids sat on the floor in front of their parents' chairs, pushing bright yellow dump trucks or putting together wooden puzzles of cartoon characters. Children my age or older sat with their parents and read magazines; others stared at the tropical fish in the tank or out the windows.

All that day, I'd studied everyone and everything I'd seen at Children's. I'd stared at all of the needles, nurses, and strange medical machines. In the bright room, I again found myself staring, delaying my blinks, and watching the other kids waiting to see a doctor.

I sat across from a mother and her son. The boy was a few years older than me; fifteen or sixteen, I guessed. He had a dark complexion like his mother. But what really got me was how natural and healthy the boy looked, even though he had a bald head. He didn't even wear a hat. Mom noticed, too. After checking in, she sat by me, leaned over, and said, "Your head could look just as good as his, Jase."

No sooner had my parents taken their seats, when a nurse called, "Chad!" and the boy and his mother stood and followed the nurse through a door.

In a while, it was our turn to go back and see the doctor. I was ready to leave. Despite all the bright colors in this room, the problems of these other waiting kids were gloomy, sad, and pressed a gray feeling against me.

Their struggle and sickness rested on the tip of my tongue, but I couldn't talk about it yet. I hadn't really experienced the disease or its cure. I was not bald and had no dark circles beneath my eyes. And, I didn't feel particularly different than I had the month or year before. I knew I had cancer, but only because someone told me so.

I didn't understand what it'd take to turn the "me" that I saw in a mirror into the image of these other kids. I didn't belong with the kids at my grade school anymore, but I didn't belong with the kids here either. I was just hanging out, made to stand in some wobbly spot where an old life and a new life bashed together. A gut feeling told me that I'd soon have the same problems as those kids in the waiting room. But right then, the gap was still there, and I was glad. I was thankful to still have my hair, to still look healthy, and to be leaving the waiting room.

The nurse who rescued us guided my parents and me along one hallway, around a corner, and into another hallway that bustled like a hall at school just after the mid-morning bell. I'd never seen anything like it before. It was like a scene from *The Wizard of Oz* gone chemo; a scene starring happy, hairless munchkins.

I walked down this long, narrow, white hallway full of scrambling adults and children. It was patterned with doors, each leading to a separate examining room, and each exam room was occupied by a family. Nurses and doctors quickly moved from one exam room to the next. Some of the young patients were actually spray-

IV Stand, Skateboards, and Prosthetic Leg Sword Fights

ing the medical staff with water—some used squirt guns, others used extra-large syringes, which worked well when the needle was pulled off. Some kids were practicing wheelies in their wheelchairs. Others used IV stands as skateboards, rolling up and down the hallway. I passed an examining room where I saw a kid blowing up a rubber glove like a party balloon, and in another I even saw two kids sword-fighting with their prosthetic limbs. Imagine seeing a couple of patients hopping around dueling with plastic legs—one leg had a tube sock with red bands at the top, the other still wore both a sock and shoe. I was horrified and fascinated.

"Holy cow," I mumbled.

The nurse walked my parents and me through sword-fighting and flying water like it was no big deal; this was just another normal day at work for her. We followed close behind, practically hanging on her white coattails. There was a stunning difference between the craziness in this hallway and the solemn doctors' offices in Missoula, or, for that matter, the quiet waiting room we'd just left. By this time I was totally overwhelmed, thinking and feeling so many things that it was as if I felt nothing.

We followed the nurse to a scale where she weighed me, then kept going down the bustling hallway until we reached its end. She turned on the light in the very last examining room; the only empty room.

"Here we are!" she said.

Mom and Dad thanked the nurse. Still stunned and silent, I waved instead. She accepted my effort with a smile, and then said that funny phrase nurses often say:

"The doctor will be right with you."

This isn't true. It's just a saying that goes with the white uniform and thermometer. "The doctor will be right with you," or "It will just be a little poke," or "This won't hurt a bit," are all white lies hiding behind big smiles. It's never just a little poke, and it always hurts more than a bit. I wasn't fooled. I knew "The doctor would NOT be right with us."

Doctors have a lot to deal with every day, especially on Tuesdays, in Bone Tumor Clinic. I soon learned that the doctors at Children's Hospital treated all different kinds of cancer and had become so busy that they needed to allocate certain days of the week to specific types of cancer. Tuesday was the day set aside for people with cancers like mine; the giant need for healing meant a long wait before seeing a doctor.

The hospital staff did what they could to help during the wait. They left fun things to play with. There were games and small toys in a cupboard just below each examining table. The toys were mostly for kids smaller than me, but who wants to play with any toy when there are stethoscopes, rubber gloves, and blood pressure pumps lying around?

Mom scolded me. "Don't play with the doctor's tools!" she said.

"No one's gonna know, Mom!" I protested.

Of course, about that time, somebody knocked and the door suddenly opened. I about jumped out of my skin. There I was, wearing a set of rubber gloves, with a stethoscope dangling from my neck. I was squeezing the bulb on a blood pressure pump, and sitting in the chair usually reserved for the doctor. Not only one, but two of them walked in.

"Interesting stuff, huh?" said the first doctor. He was slim. Tall and slender, his arms, fingers, and even his nose were thin.

"Yep! We get to play with that stuff all day, every day," said the other man. This doctor scratched his peppered gray beard and took a seat next to Mom. His gray slacks, as well as his shirt and tie were pressed, and his hair was neatly combed and parted down one side. The dark brown and gray in his trimmed beard matched his hair perfectly. He introduced himself as Dr. Pendergrass, and shook hands with both my parents.

I took off the rubber gloves and stethoscope, and he shook my hand firmly as well.

"Nice to meet you, Jason," Dr. Pendergrass said and, looking at the other doctor, he added, "This is Dr. Conrad."

The taller, slimmer man pushed his glasses up the bridge of his nose with his index finger. Dr. Conrad's simple, wire-framed glasses seemed to fit his narrow face and build. He was younger than Dr. Pendergrass and clean-shaven, though he wasn't as neatly pressed. His tie was loose and the top button on his white dress shirt was undone. Dr. Conrad's shirt was a little wrinkly and untucked in back. His hair looked like he had combed it that morning, but I could see that between the morning and our appointment, there had been a long and busy day.

He also shook each of our hands, "Dr. Conrad. Pleased to meet you," he said politely, hopping up onto the examining table where I should've been sitting.

"Jason." My attention turned back to Dr. Pendergrass. "We're here to help you beat this thing."

I learned that Dr. Pendergrass would be the head oncologist. He'd make the decisions about when, how, and how much chemotherapy. Something he called my "protocol."

"For the time being, you need to stay at Children's, so I can keep a close eye on you," Dr. Pendergrass said. "But it won't be too long before you can go home and have some treatments if you'd like. Once everyone gets a little more settled into the protocol, Dr. Speckart, your oncologist at home in Montana, can take it from there."

Dr. Conrad had a softer voice and talked less than Dr. Pendergrass. He told us that he was an orthopedic surgeon. He was in charge of operating on my shoulder.

"If any more tumors grow on your bones, I'll surgically remove the cancer," Dr. Conrad explained.

The doctors were smart. They knew all about cancer. They were patient too; they never talked over my head. There was nothing that Dr. Pendergrass and Dr. Conrad said to my parents that they didn't also say to me. They wanted us to really believe that I could live, grow up, and leave cancer behind me.

"Ewing's is a rare disease, Jason, but breakthroughs happen every day, so statistics and war stories about Ewing's will probably be frightening and just plain inaccurate," Dr. Pendergrass said. "If your parents run off to the library and start reading about cancer, would you remind them that a book published even one year ago could be misleading?"

My parents smiled and so did Dr. Pendergrass.

"What I want you to understand is: this is beatable," he said.

After that, I guess the doctors thought we were feeling pretty good, and they went on about possible risks and side effects. Dr. Pendergrass and Dr. Conrad told us all about chemo drugs with big long names, and about nausea, anti-nausea, white

IV Stand, Skateboards, and Prosthetic Leg Sword Fights

blood cells, red blood cells, and platelets. The syllables describing disease and treatment were endless.

I didn't get everything, but I did have a better idea of what was happening. I liked both doctors and trusted them already. I was way more secure about my disease and the cure I'd need to survive it. Dr. Conrad and Dr. Pendergrass next took away that security just as fast as they had provided it. We had some tough decisions to make alone, decisions they couldn't make for us.

Chapter Seven

Bones from a Cadaver

"Wait a minute," I said, "you're gonna put someone else's bone in my body? You guys have spares lying around or something?"

Dr. Conrad and Dr. Pendergrass had laid out a series of treatment choices. Dr. Pendergrass told us about certain combinations of drugs that would probably be effective, and wouldn't make me as sick. He also told us we could be part of a study. The study was a much more aggressive approach. It was made up of an experimental set of chemo drugs, a combination that'd make the time I spent in treatment more difficult, but it gave me a better chance of surviving cancer.

Dr. Conrad also gave me a choice about the major shoulder surgery I needed to have. He told me that during my biopsy in Missoula, the tumor on my collarbone had been removed and the bone had been rigorously scraped in an attempt to get rid of the entire tumor. However, Dr. Conrad believed the collarbone needed to be taken out of my body. I could choose to just have my bone removed, or I could have my bone removed and a donor bone put in its place.

I was listening, paying attention to all that the doctors were telling me, but my head was full. I was beginning to feel a step behind as information blew past me. Then, *Smack!* it hit me. The thought of someone else's bone in my body stuck in my head.

Dr. Conrad answered my question about spare body parts lying around, "It's called an allograft, Jason," he replied.

"Oh, great, throw another humongous word on the pile that means nothing to me," I said, knowing that I'd never get away with sassing like that at home or school.

I wasn't angry at the doctor. I was frustrated because I didn't understand, and I was tired of keeping quiet and letting all these decisions happen around me. This was my body, not the doctors' and not my parents'. So I spoke up. And right then I became a part of my own treatment.

Dr. Conrad hopped off of the examining table and put his hand on my bandaged shoulder.

He knelt so that we were eye to eye. Then he pressed on the outside of my shoulder.

"You have one growth plate here, Jason," he said, then slid his long fingers down the bandages that still remained. He pressed hard, following my collarbone to its end, just below my Adam's apple.

"And another growth plate here," he continued.

Dr. Conrad told me that if I wanted the allograft, my bone would be sawed off on the insides of the two growth plates. He would remove the majority of my bone and replace it with a bone from a donor.

"When you do beat this thing, you're going to need those two plates to grow big and strong, Jason," he said.

I looked at him, then at my parents.

"We'll leave you alone to talk about your choices. Take as long as you need. We'll check in on you soon," Dr. Conrad said.

Both doctors stood and started to walk out the door, leaving the three of us to think about what they'd said, and try and decide what to do.

"Wait!" I called.

The two doctors turned around just before leaving the examining room.

"You're gonna saw my bone on both ends, and then take it out of my body?" I asked.

"Yes," Dr. Conrad answered.

"You're gonna put a bone that's been sawed from someone else's body, and then donated to the hospital, inside my body?" I asked.

This time, Dr. Pendergrass chimed in with Dr. Conrad, "Yes," they answered together.

"And what's going to keep the sawed donor bone inside the hole between my two growth plates?" I asked.

Dr. Conrad took a step toward me.

"We'll use a long, stainless steel plate and a series of screws. The plate and the screws will run along the donor bone, attaching it to your growth plates," he answered.

"Like plumber's tape," Dr. Pendergrass added.

"Oh, plumber's tape?" I mumbled.

The two doctors started to leave again, closing the door behind them.

"Wait!" I said again.

The door crept back open, and both men peeked inside.

"Have you ever done this surgery before?" I asked.

"Not exactly," Dr. Conrad answered.

"Do you have any more questions, Jason?"

"I don't know…not exactly…no…I don't think so?" I answered, shaking my head.

The doctors slipped out before I had a chance to change my mind.

The door clicked behind them. I kept on looking at the place where the two men had stood. *Chemotherapy intensity, recycled body parts, and stainless steel plates and screws!* Two weeks ago, I couldn't decide which pair of socks to wear. I put my boxer shorts on inside-out half the time, and my parents wouldn't let me go into the video store alone because they thought I might choose an "inappropriate" movie.

"What the hell happened to my life?" I accidentally said out loud.

Instantly, I regretted letting a curse word slip from my lips. Mom instinctively reached over and clipped my mouth with the back of her hand.

"Jason! You watch your language."

Bones from a Cadaver

Her voice started out stern and mom-like, but became a whisper by the end of her scolding. I imagined that by then she was wondering, *What the hell happened to our life?*

"What do you think, son?" Dad asked.

"Dunno, Dad," I answered.

I was fibbing. I really did know. I knew my decisions as soon as Dr. Pendergrass and Dr. Conrad explained the choices. Just underneath this present moment was the memory of the home and life I left behind—I wanted it back. I knew the surest route was to choose the most aggressive drugs and surgery. I covered the truth with hesitation because there was another memory just below this present moment: the memory of children at the McDonald House and in the hospital waiting room. I still stood outside of cancer and chemo, and didn't want to step inside of their world.

I could fool myself because a head of hair and a body that still looked healthy hid my disease. But I was moments from admitting I was sick. It was on the tip of my tongue, waiting to jerk me from a confusing, unclear place between the life I'd known and this new, different life in Seattle. It was going to be downright hard to say it out loud, but deciding on a treatment helped me own up to having a disease; it gave some specifics and detail to the sickness surrounding me, to my world with cancer.

About twenty minutes later, Dr. Conrad and Dr. Pendergrass came back in the examining room. Neither said a word. There were a few uncomfortable seconds of silence.

My stomach filled with butterflies, and without asking Mom and Dad, I talked first.

"I wanna do the study…and…having someone else's bone replace my bad one…well…I guess…that's okay, too."

Once I told the doctors, things didn't seem so wobbly and unclear. They called it a protocol, I called it having a plan, and I was all in; I was hopeful and afraid. This wasn't like getting mad about a bully calling me a name on the playground. It wasn't a meeting at the bike-racks after school where maybe somebody ended up with a bloody nose. This was big time. Now I was really going to fight.

* * * * *

It was back in second grade. I couldn't read for nothing, so I decided to stay an extra year. It made sense to me, and my teacher thought it was a good idea, too. The only problem: I forgot to tell Mom and Dad. So there I was in the principal's office at my grade school, sitting on a couch next to my teacher.

"Did you know that Jason has decided to be in the second grade for a second time?" the principal asked my mother into a phone receiver.

Needless to say, Mom was surprised. But Mom, Dad, the principal, and my teacher got it all figured out. I ended up staying in second grade for another year, and I didn't get in any trouble for not remembering to ask, even though it created a little to-do.

It'd been a few years since both second grades, and you might agree that picking a treatment was a slightly more serious choice, but my parents went along with it just the same. To be honest, when it came to deciding, I think Mom and Dad were relieved that I blurted out an answer. Maybe they saw it as a sign, or maybe they were thinking the exact same thing and I just got it out first.

Either way, Dr. Pendergrass started explaining the study's protocol. He told me that I'd have two treatments every month, for eighteen months: the first would be a five-day treatment and the second, a three-day treatment. He told me I'd start the treatment cycle right away.

"The sooner we begin, the sooner you'll be finished," Dr. Pendergrass said.

He spoke right to me, frequently stopping, looking at my parents and asking, "You still with me?"

Dr. Conrad leaned against the examining table with a manila folder in one hand and his other tucked comfortably in his pocket. He listened, waiting until Dr. Pendergrass had finished talking about chemotherapy protocol. When Dr. Pendergrass finished, Dr. Conrad said only a few words.

"We'll schedule the allograft for the summer sometime," he said.

Because it was mid-April, "the summer sometime" felt far away. Beginning my first five-day chemo treatment sank surgery to the bottom of my list of worries.

The doctors made sure I understood that there'd be no shortcut, or easy way to overcome the disease. Although, I was happy to learn that there'd always be success in the small steps along the way. There'd be that simple, quiet feeling of winning when I made it through each day.

"It's best to live day-to-day and step-by-step. Looking only to the short term leads to encouragement instead of frustration or disappointment," Dr. Pendergrass said. "Cancer has a way of breaking promises, doesn't it, Chappie?"

"It does," Dr. Conrad answered.

Dr. Conrad looked at me, "Everyone around here calls me Chappie. Even my patients," he explained, "I suppose you'd better, too."

Dr. Pendergrass ended our first visit to Clinic by telling me that I'd be having a small surgery.

Not again, I thought. The last time I had a small surgery, my life changed kind of unexpectedly.

"Regular IVs can't be used to administer chemotherapy over long periods of time," Dr. Pendergrass told us. "If an IV is used, chemotherapy drugs would break down your veins. Leaks could also occur, which would result in severe burns to the skin because of the potency of chemotherapy."

He told us that to fix these problems, somebody had invented a device that was small and round, about the size of a silver dollar. They were going to put the device just under my skin on the right side of my chest. It had a tube that would run from the small circle to a vein, which led directly to my heart. The device was called a port-a-cath, or "port" for short. And just like the port or harbor of a city, the port would be the going-in and going-out point for all of the medical "everythings" entering and leaving my body. A needle would poke the little circle just below my skin anytime drugs needed to be pushed in, or blood pulled out. Like nails on a chalkboard, or seeing my own blood on gauze at the dentist's, the thought of a device implanted under my skin made me squirm. But the small surgery was worthwhile compared to broken veins and burns from chemo.

Chemotherapy was going to start right after surgery, which meant I should prepare for a week-long hospital stay. I wasn't looking forward to being readmitted to a hospital, but I was glad this appointment was finally over.

The bustling hallway outside our examining room had quieted. Many of the other examining rooms were empty, each of their lights switched off. We wound our way back to the clinic's waiting room and I noticed there were still a few kids in the chairs or playing on the floor. Once again, I noticed their sickness, but this time, I felt the gap between us closing.

It didn't take long to get back to the McDonald House. The house and Children's Hospital were practically across the street from one another. Although they were close, and I'd only left one building full of cancer patients to travel to another full of cancer patients, I realized how very different they were. The McDonald House was like recess when compared to the "white castle on the hill." At the house, there'd be no one to poke me with needles or to push on my shoulder. There'd be no drugs to make me sick or reports of poor health. It was just a house full of people facing the same awful problems, enjoying a brief rest before returning to Children's.

My time outside of the hospital was short, and in a blink I was preparing for the small surgery and my first chemotherapy treatment. I sat in another waiting room at Children's, waiting to get into another hospital gown and have another surgery. My days seemed to be stuck on fast-forward. Leaving the hospital in Montana, the McDonald House, sitting in Clinic, leaving, then returning to Children's for surgery and chemo: it all blurred together in a line of swiftly passing time.

Chapter Eight

The Art of Throwing Up

"You must be an athlete," a nurse said softly.

I didn't recognize her voice or know what she was talking about—and I didn't really care.

"You have a strong heartbeat," she said.

IVs and anesthetics had brought me from a waiting room in the morning to a hospital bed in the evening. Sickness and a nurse taking my blood pressure woke me. A dim light shining behind the nurse outlined her sturdy frame and curly hair.

I didn't reply. Cotton-mouthed from the drugs and dry hospital air, I had a hard time prying my lips apart and peeling my tongue from the roof of my mouth. I barely had the energy to lift my eyelids, much less pry, peel, and come out with an answer.

The nurse again broke the silence. She stripped the blood pressure cuff from my arm, and followed the familiar sound of Velcro pulling apart with another question.

"Would you like to start chemo treatments tonight or wait until tomorrow?" she asked.

Silence was no longer an option. I was pressed to make a decision, to answer the nurse.

"Tomorrow," I croaked.

Not wanting to talk more than that, I closed my eyes.

The next thing I heard was the whining sound of some kind of small engine, and then the same nurse's voice from the night before. I looked around. It was morning now, and I knew there was no more delaying treatment. The nurse was starting chemotherapy. She tugged on the newest addition to my body, my Port. I looked under my hospital gown.

I saw a small bump pushing out from my chest. The bump stuck out about a finger width, gradually bowing up, and then flattening at the top. Just like Dr. Pendergrass said, it reminded me of a thick silver dollar, covered by a thin coating of skin. A needle poked from my skin on the crown of the bump. The needle was covered by a clear piece of plastic, and was attached to a long tube. My eyes followed the tube, which followed my arm through the sleeve on my hospital gown. It connected me to an IV bag, which was filled with a dark liquid. *So that's what chemo looks like.*

The whining engine, the nurse, the sight of my Port, and the medicine that began to run through my body didn't bug me much. I fell back to sleep before the nurse had finished fiddling with my IV pole. But I didn't sleep much longer.

My eyes flew open. There was a terrible ache in my bones and strong burning in my stomach. The burning moved to a sharp pain. Without thinking, my hands shot out for a nearby hospital bucket and I puked. It was my first puke of the day, but it certainly wouldn't be my last. My stomach ached and the room spun each time I cracked an eyelid. I'd had the flu before, and I'd been sick just the previous night from anesthetic. Chemo was worse, believe me, way worse.

I shut my eyes again to keep the spinning down, and I buried my face deep in the hospital bucket. I was waiting for the sickness to pass when my attention was unexpectedly yanked from the bucket.

"If you keep your head tipped up a bit, it'll keep it from coming out your nose," said a voice from across the room.

I opened one eye and turned my head from the bucket. I scanned the room in an effort to locate the person who was attached to this advice. There were two other kids in the room, but I really only noticed one of them.

Finally, I could see a little better. I opened my other eye, and focused in on a boy who sat on the edge of the bed opposite mine. His skinny legs were too short to touch the floor, so they were left to dangle just above it. He had a grin on his face and held a large remote controller in his hand. The controller was steering a miniature monster truck. He skillfully guided the truck, bumping its hood into my IV pole. I recognized the whiny engine noise that the truck made; it was part of the reason why I woke up a while ago.

The boy controlling the truck was also familiar. He was the kid with the dark complexion and nice-shaped head that my mother and I noticed at our visit to Clinic.

"If you keep your head tipped up, the throw-up won't burn your nose as much," he said again.

The boy hopped down from the bed. "Hey, man. I'm Chad, and I am an expert in the art of throwing up," he said.

Chad's mother sat in a chair next to his bed. They looked very much alike, sharing facial features and a dark complexion. She ran her hand across her forehead, brushing her straight, black hair away from her eyes.

"And I'm Chad's mom, Cherié," she said, "Welcome to Children's."

"Jason," I said, attempting to introduce myself but getting only my name out in between heaves.

My nausea and spins quit long enough to talk with Chad. I noticed that, unlike me, he wasn't wearing a hospital gown. Chad had on flannel shorts, high-top basketball shoes, and a white T-shirt that read "Corvette." His clothes hung loosely on his lean frame. Even his eyeglasses looked a tad big sitting on his face, like maybe they'd been fitted before losing loads of weight.

He was skinny—legs, arms, and torso, but his legs were overly so. There were scars

The Art of Throwing Up

on the lower parts of both of his legs; later I'd learn that portions of each calf muscle had been removed with his tumors.

With a bit of a strut, Chad walked toward his mother. He picked up a folding chair from beside her and moved it across the room. Chad wanted to talk but didn't want to bother any other patients. He put the chair next to my bed and sat down.

We talked about our doctors and the hospital.

"Hey man, the doctors won't tell ya, but you don't need to wear a hospital gown, unless you like showing off your butt, that is," he advised. Soon I discovered he was a fountain of advice: "Never eat the hospital food. Bring your own snacks. Cold cereal's best because there's lots of choices. Once you eat a box during treatment and throw it up for a week, you'll never want it again...cereal is good when you gotta blow groceries 'cause you can just move on, try a new one every time. I've been through most of 'em, have to keep an eye out for commercials advertising new flavors. Oh yeah...and Kool-Aid, it tastes the same going down as it does comin' back up...I swear."

Chad told me he was sixteen years old, and had just gotten his driver's license. We talked about our hometowns. Chad told me that he was from Twisp, Washington, and when Missoula, Montana, became a topic, a jolly voice from across the room chimed in.

A boy pulled back a curtain which surrounded the bed next to mine. A curtain was the only thing that allowed any privacy in the room the three of us shared. As soon as we made eye contact, the boy exclaimed, "I'm from Montana, too!"

It was as if he couldn't keep this fact inside any longer or he'd burst.

"Travis is my name," he said with an abrupt nod. "I'm from Havre, Montana."

He practically leapt out of bed, and hastily started toward Chad and me. Travis walked fast, clumsily, and he nearly fell face down on the hospital floor—causing his "Seattle Mariner's" baseball cap to fall off. The loss of his baseball cap revealed his bald head, as well as a bright pink scar that ran along the side of his scalp.

Travis pulled his IV pole beside him, as if it were second nature, as if it was a buddy he brought with him everywhere. He was smiling so big that his plump cheeks bulged, leaving only two small slits for his brown eyes. Like me, he wore a hospital gown. He also wore white gym socks, but the tops were down around his ankles and they didn't help Travis's traction as he hurried across the room.

Politely, Travis held out a slightly pudgy hand for me to shake. He made me smile. I loved meeting Travis, Chad, and Cherié, but sickness soon returned and my smile was gone again. Once more, a fire began to burn in my stomach. My lips pursed and my eyes opened so wide that their edges must've been revealed. Chad saw the change in my face, grabbed a bucket from beside my bed, and handed it to me.

This time while puking, I tried to keep my head "tipped up a bit," so throw-up wouldn't come out of my nose. My heaving, coughing, and spitting didn't affect the conversation between Chad and Travis. They went on chatting even while I was making all that noise. Even though I wanted to, I couldn't keep talking with them. I was sick and my bones ached. I needed to lie back and close my eyes.

I found that throwing up is hard work. I was exhausted for most of the hospital stay. I kept my eyes closed for the majority of the five-day treatment, opening them just long enough to find a bucket. The bucket was always the same, but many times the people who handed it to me were different. My mother, father, brother, Grandma, or Grandpa took turns sitting beside my bed. People often moved in and out of the room, but, day or night, I was never alone; there was always a family member next to my bed.

Throwing up happened so often that I stopped having to say anything; all that was required was a raised hand. I'd simply raise my hand, like I was asking a question at school, and someone would give me a bucket.

One evening I rolled to the side of my bed and threw my arm in the air. It was only seconds before I was handed a bucket. I recognized the hand immediately. It belonged to my Grandma Dorie, and when the sickness passed, I rolled over to talk to her.

Grandma Dorie sat with her usual straight posture, looking presentable, even though she'd been seated in an uncomfortable chair for hours.

"Hi, Gram," I said, weakly.

"Well, are you feeling any better?" she asked.

"Yeah, for a few minutes anyway," I answered.

There was repetition in my sickness. A short delight followed every bout of vomiting. For a few minutes after puking I felt good, or normal, or at least less terrible than seconds before, when I thought my left foot was going to flip inside out and spring from my throat.

I'd have my short break from nausea, but sickness would again creep up, forcing me to curl into a ball, hold my stomach, and close my eyes. Hopefully, I could fall asleep for a while, before raising my hand once again.

It was a cruel cycle, but I knew I had a few good moments to talk to my grandma before needing to puke. Grandma Dorie began to tell me a story. She told me that Grandpa Harp had been sitting in one of the hospital hallways and had met another boy's grandpa. Neither one of the grandpas was shy, so the two men began to talk.

Grandma paused, "You know how your grandfather is," she said. I nodded.

The other grandpa also had a grandson at Children's. The boy's name was Erik, he was fifteen, a little older than me, but he had the same exact type of cancer that I had. My grandma also told me we needed to pray for Erik, because he was much sicker than me. Grandma Dorie kept talking about the boy, but I stopped listening. My nausea rose once again. Thankfully, as Grandma talked, I began to fall asleep. But before I slept, I thought of Erik and prayed.

Jesus, please help Erik's medicine work…Amen.

* * * * *

A Look Back: Chemo

With respect to cancer, and with respect to life, the more I learn, the more I realize how much I still do not know. Answered questions only create an empty space, a bit of room to be filled by more questions. Inside Children's Hospital, dire circumstance had been awakened, and truly dire questions were roused inside of me—doubts had replaced daydreams and fear replaced fable. New uncertainty, information, and experience came at an overwhelming speed, especially at the beginning of treatment.

Back then I attached a great deal of understanding to the "Yes," given to me by Dr. Speckart when I asked if there was a cure, and the "Yes," given to me by Uncle Greg when I asked if that cure would hurt. I began to understand the torment that would cause my appearance to be

The Art of Throwing Up

similar to the bald-headed peers at Children's Hospital and the McDonald House.

The creation of my life, my disease, the cure to survive my disease, and the side effects of the cure, all mingled inside of me. The process of one cell becoming two is a cycle that begins upon conception, and ends upon death. Without this cycle I would not only cease to be, I would never have been. Cells gathered to form an infant heart, lung, eyes, nose, and toes. And to continue my life, the reproduction of cells remains necessary to carry oxygen, clot blood, fight infection, grow hair, and line the organs that make up the body's many systems.

When a cell is given the signal to reproduce, it begins a cycle of four phases: It synthesizes proteins and manufactures DNA. DNA is then doubled and the cell prepares and undergoes mitosis. Once an exact replica of the parent cell is generated, it splits, becoming two daughter cells. The daughter cells rest before beginning the cycle once again.

When abnormal cells earnestly undergo the same fundamental life cycle, they build tumors instead of organs and promise death instead of life. The treatment given in an attempt to save my life came from an agent that had brought death to millions of soldiers in World War I. Cells gone wrong caused my disease, war gone wrong allowed me to fight it.

Nitrogen mustard, commonly known as "mustard gas," was a chemical agent used heavily during World War I. In World War II, several soldiers were accidentally exposed to the gas. Later, blood tests showed that the exposed soldiers had suppressed white blood cell counts. Because both white blood cells and cancer cells rapidly reproduce, researchers believed there was a correlation between the death of white cells and that of cancer cells. Patients were given nitrogen mustard, not in the form of gas, but intravenously. Their improvement was remarkable, but also temporary. None of the patients receiving the treatment at that time lived to tell the tale. However, researchers began to study substances that might have similar effects on cancer cells. Success followed—a chemical weapon turned out to be a misunderstood tyrant. Two of the five drugs in my chemotherapy protocol were nitrogen mustards.

In its simplest definition, chemotherapy is treating cancer with the use of drugs. Chemotherapy drugs, also called anticancer drugs, are designed to interfere with the cell cycle. Different anticancer drugs work in various ways: some attack cells at specific phases of the cell cycle while others are not phase-specific, but inhibit and kill a cell throughout the cycle. Doctors create a chemotherapy protocol by compiling anticancer drugs that will attack cancer cells at different times and in different ways, thus ensuring the best possible chance to rid the body of all cancer. Each anticancer drug is unique, each poses a different threat to cancer, but all directly or indirectly effect a cell's DNA, and all are toxic.

While I was in the hospital for my first treatment, I learned what "toxic" meant, and began to understand the definition of "poison." Chemotherapy causes nausea, neutropenia, anemia, inability to stop bleeding, hair loss, mouth sores, bone and joint pain, and fatigue. It can also cause an irregular heartbeat or possible heart failure, loss of reflexes, and flat-footedness. During my first five-day treatment, I experienced many of these effects, and would eventually know all of them intimately.

The nausea came mostly from chemotherapy's effect on two specific parts of my brain. These parts of the brain note that there is poison in the body, and they signal the stomach to empty its contents. However, the poison was entering my body through the bloodstream, not through my stomach. Because it remained even after I vomited, my stomach was signaled to empty again and again.

Drugs attacking the cancer inside of me could not differentiate between normal cells and cancer cells. Any cell in the midst of the cell cycle can be affected by chemotherapy. The more a cell reproduces, the more likely it is to be destroyed. Abnormal cells multiply out of control, which makes them the most probable target. However, the cells made in the bone marrow (red and white blood cells, as well as platelets) are also particularly affected. As my treatment progressed, I became neutropenic as a result of the chemotherapy which had depleted my white blood cells; I could no longer fight off infection. When there were too few red blood cells to carry an adequate amount of oxygen throughout my body, I would become anemic and suffer from extreme fatigue. Also, because the body uses platelets to clot blood, with these cells being depleted, any bleeding would be difficult to stop.

Other cells that reproduce rapidly would be affected, such as those that make hair, therefore causing hair loss. Cells lining my mouth and digestive system would also be harmed, resulting in irritating mouth sores, and additional nausea and discomfort from the lack of cells coating the stomach, esophagus, and intestines.

Chemotherapy directly affects muscles, nerves, and ligaments, causing additional weakness as well as the pain I felt in my bones and joints. There were also long-term effects from my treatment. Flat-footedness made my left foot permanently turn in. I would lose deep tendon reflexes, which meant that when I sat on an examining table, and the doctor hit my knee with that funny triangle hammer, my leg would not move. The muscles in my heart would also be damaged, which would cause it to weaken, and maybe someday fail.

The long-term side effects of chemotherapy sound the most discouraging, but the very fact that I am fortunate enough to enjoy them today makes them good problems. Many other children fighting cancer, and their parents, hope and pray that they, or their child, might one day suffer the effects that come from surviving cancer. A list of chemotherapy's side effects, both short-term and long-term, along with an understanding of their specifics and texture, gives good reason to despise the treatment. However, it is important to keep in mind that chemotherapy was not given to increase comfort or improve the quality of life—it was administered to prevent my death.

Chapter Nine

A Wish is Granted

The cycle of sickness, sleep, then sickness again continued hour after hour, night and day. However, in the break of each morning there was a strange and unexpected gift. When the sun stretched and the city yawned, these moments of reprieve seemed longer, and moments of curling, holding, and throwing up seemed shorter.

One morning, sunlight coming from the hospital window woke me. It was a welcomed alarm clock because I knew that morning would leave me feeling stronger and less sick. I lifted my head and opened my eyes. Several people stood in my corner of the room. People I didn't recognize surrounded my bed.

I noticed a boy sitting in a wheelchair at the foot of my bed. Like Chad, he was also older than me and didn't wear a hospital gown. He wore sweatpants, a black hooded sweatshirt, and slippers that looked warm and comfortable. The boy was skinny and pale. His face was thin; his skin pulled tightly against his jaw and high cheekbones. I could see he was tall, even though he was sitting, because of how his legs bent awkwardly in the wheelchair.

When he noticed I was awake, a smile bloomed. It lit up his white skin, and set in motion a wake of wrinkles that traveled up his forehead and on to his shiny scalp. This was Erik, the boy my grandma told me about, the one who was sicker than me and needed us to pray for him.

Erik and the other people around my bed joked and laughed, acting as though our families had been friends for twenty years.

"Good morning, Jason," Mom said.

"Good morning, Jason," a chatter of unfamiliar voices repeated.

"Good morning?" I replied.

While I was sleeping and puking, my parents and grandparents had met and had long talks with other families in the hospital. They'd bonded in hallways and the cafeteria. They'd had conversations about medical protocol, and one another's lives.

Mom and Dad had already visited Erik's room a number of times, and Erik's mother and father had also visited Chad and me in this room. All I'd known since chemo started was the repetition and cycle of sickness. I had no idea who was coming or going. I remembered my grandmother's story about Erik and how the two grandpas met in the hallway. Even so, Grandpa Harp took it upon himself to tell me again.

"In the hallway, Jason, can you believe that?" my grandfather said, while gently punching my non-bandaged shoulder.

"Cool, Gramps," I answered.

Between Grandpa Harp and my mother, I shuddered to think of all the things that these strangers already knew about me. I also shuddered to think of the approaching moment when my sickness would return, and these nice people would be forced to view my left foot being lost into a bucket. Surprisingly, I felt better than I had during the past several days. Reaching to my right, I pushed the "Up" button on the controller attached to my bed.

The bed bent forward, and I knew every inch was a gamble. Except when using a urinal or puke bucket, I'd barely moved since the five-day treatment started. I had no idea how my stomach would react, but curiosity outweighed caution: I wanted to know what was happening in my corner of the hospital. Erik watched the bed rise, examining the expression on my face and understanding the gamble. He didn't offer advice or jokes like Chad. Erik looked more reserved or shy. But when I sat up straight, he again smiled, applauding me.

From my new vantage point I could see a small dog on Erik's lap. He rolled his wheelchair next to my bed, putting the dog close enough for me to pet. It had long fur and a squished face. I reached over and scratched its head.

Erik's mother and father stood behind his wheelchair.

"I'm Sheri, this is Rick. And this is our son Erik," his mother said. "Oh...and Erik calls the dog Chappie."

Sheri spoke softly, and I had to strain to hear her. Her shoulder-length hair was blonde, especially curly from a perm, I think, and she nervously reached up to fidget with an earring.

I paused and thought for a moment.

Puzzled, I asked, "Like the doctor?"

Erik nodded.

"My doctor was named after a dog?" I said, in disbelief.

Surprised by my question, Rick smiled and even laughed out loud a little. He looked very much like an older version of Erik. They shared high cheekbones, a thin face, and Rick was also bald on top. (Although, he was bald from age, not chemotherapy. Or, as Chad would describe him, "Bald by natural causes.")

"Erik named the dog after your doctor," Rick chuckled.

Just then somebody switched on a TV that had been placed between Chad's bed and mine and Erik was now focused on the screen. Across the room, Chad's eyes were also glued to the TV. Further challenging my nausea, I looked at the screen as the picture switched from static to a home video. Nearly everyone took a step closer.

Everybody really wants to see what's coming on that TV, I thought.

Erik's mother didn't step toward the television. Instead Sheri moved near my bed.

"This recording's from Erik's Make-A-Wish," she told me.

"What's Make-A-Wish?" I asked.

I learned that Make-A-Wish is an organization which gives wishes to critically ill children. Erik's wish was to be on the television show *Cheers*. He hadn't been on the show yet, but he'd gotten to meet part of the cast. John Ratzenberger, who played the part of Cliff the mailman, had visited Erik at Children's. Erik's family recorded the visit and now shared it with Chad and Cherié, my family and me.

"So there're some good things about having cancer?" I asked.

Sheri looked at me, her lips and her voice quivering so slightly it was almost undetectable, "Well…if I had to make a list…the bad list would be very bad, but very short, and the good list would be long and continues to grow," she answered.

* * * * *

A Look Back: Erik and His Family

In many ways Erik's family and much of his childhood might be the kind of idealistic life a person daydreams about. It was full of love, laughter, a strong faith, and a great deal of family time together in a summer home on a lake.

Erik was born in 1975, the third of Rick and Sheri's four sons. Erik and his siblings: Geoff, Ryan, and younger brother Jonathan, grew up in Sedro-Woolley, Washington. However, summers were spent at a cabin on Big Lake, just about twenty miles from their house in town. As the years passed, the whole family would move to the lake on the day that school was let out in the spring, and would not return to Sedro-Woolley until the first day of school in fall. This yearly escape was tradition from the time Erik and his brother were toddlers, to the summers spent with high-school crushes and first loves as they grew into young men—memories at the lake help describe Erik's family more than anything.

When the boys were very young and building sand castles on the beach that bordered Big Lake, Erik's grandfather would pay them a nickel for any pieces of broken glass that they unearthed and picked up. One summer, the old man found Erik behind the garage breaking glass bottles with a hammer, and interrupted his plan to collect more than just a few nickels.

At Big Lake, our nation's independence is not celebrated on the 4th of July, but a day earlier, on the 3rd, when a professional fireworks display bursts from a raft on the center of the lake, and less formal fireworks are lit all around its shore. Why it's celebrated a day early there, I am not certain, but the barbecues and ski boats that fill Big Lake on the 3rd rival any 4th of July celebration.

Life looked different for Erik and his family when he was diagnosed with Ewing's Sarcoma. It was not the life for which they had planned or dreamt. However, when a difficulty like cancer shakes a life, all that is superficial and material falls away; what remains are the perfections and imperfections of love and memory.

Although it is true that the most difficult moments in Rick and Sheri's life took place while Erik fought cancer, that time also holds their fondest memories. On the day Erik was diagnosed with cancer, his mother and father drove from Children's Hospital back to Big Lake. He spent time with his family, and though Dr. Chappie Conrad advised against it, Erik asked his dad to start up their ski boat and take him waterskiing. Later that summer, during the 3rd of July celebration, Erik was too sick to run around and shoot off fireworks with his brothers. Instead he sat in a lawn chair, and others kept him supplied with Bottle Rockets and Lady Fingers. Even with his discomfort, Erik smiled. And even as Rick and Sheri watched their son's condition worsen, witnessing his inability to have fun as he had in the past, this particular celebration remains the couple's favorite 3rd of July.

Erik had been fighting cancer for more than a year when I had been wheeled onto the second floor of Children's Hospital to begin treatment. Rick and Sheri often introduced themselves to families new to cancer and chemotherapy offering them wisdom and helpful advice. But they did not want to meet my family. Erik's health was getting worse, and because Erik and I both had been diagnosed with Ewing's Sarcoma, they did not want to frighten me or my parents. Despite their effort, we could not be kept apart. In the hallway of Children's, Erik's grandfather and Grandpa Harp met, and from there our families began to care for one another almost instantaneously.

* * * * *

I only watched the video of Erik's Make-A-Wish for a few minutes, until sickness forced me to listen to the rest with eyes closed. I could hear the actor joking with Erik. The jokes made Erik laugh on the tape, and everyone watching the video laughed along with the recording.

The video gave us a momentary escape from the hospital and an uplifting feeling. Not surprisingly, Harp was lifted higher than the rest—he wanted to make escaping the hospital a real event. He believed that getting a wish granted wasn't an everyday occurrence and used any excuse to have a good time. After watching Erik's video, he believed a celebration was in order. Harp thought that the day was a little too fine, the hospital a little too quiet, and a barbecue ought to pleasantly shake up everyone's routine.

He revved the engine under the hood of his motor home and pulled it away from the McDonald House. Grandpa Harp drove the motor home across the street and took up ten or eleven stalls in the hospital parking lot. He set up the grill.

Kids I recognized and kids I'd never seen before all walked from the hospital's front door to my Grandma Dorie and Grandpa Harp's motor home. A crowd of bald-headed children walked from the cancer ward to the parking lot. They flashed blue passes at hospital staff. The passes allowed each patient to leave the hospital for a while. Parents, siblings, grandparents, and even some nurses wheeled or walked alongside patients from the second floor. Every kid, and each of their escorts, enjoyed the very best hamburgers and hot dogs—compliments of my grandpa's grill.

I lay in the corner of my hospital room looking out the window, watching Travis, Chad, and Erik lead the other children towards the barbecue. I was too sick to attend the party, and was left behind with the less-than-appetizing hospital food—which was the motivating force sending many of the kids running to the barbecue in the first place. Seeing the disappointment on my face as the other children left our room and our floor, my father offered me a reminder.

"You should be thankful you're not as sick as many of these other kids, Jason," he said.

I was thankful, but the kids who looked so much sicker than me a few days before, didn't appear to be so on this day. *I mean, at least they're all well enough to eat real food.*

From my bed I could see the smoke from the grill and kids at the barbecue. For a moment I even thought I caught the scent of meat cooking through the window. The smell of real food was pleasant, but the thought of actually eating any type of food, hospital, barbecue, or otherwise, made my stomach turn.

A Wish is Granted

Despite my upset stomach, hamburgers and hot dogs reminded me of barbecuing at home. Though Grandma Dorie always fixed the salads, potatoes, and even the meat, Grandpa Harp would throw the meat on the grill and then take full credit for the entire meal.

"Who wants to kiss the cook?" he'd call out.

It was a funny scene that never changed and could always be counted on. I just hoped that all of those strangers out the window didn't take Harp too seriously.

Again Grandma Dorie had prepared the greens, the meat, and all the fixings. Once her job at the motor home was finished, she returned to the cancer ward and sat next to my bed. We both stared out the window at the batch of mischief that my grandfather had stirred up. I looked at the people enjoying the charcoal cloud of charm surrounding Grandpa, then I looked at Grandma, and considered how fortunate I was.

Her face had smile lines bending from each corner of her mouth, even when she wasn't smiling. Each line was evidence of joy, fond memories of our family, other barbecues, birthdays, and holidays. Like my grandmother, I hoped that the lines on my face would someday stay, even when my smile faded.

I rolled over and curled into a ball, clutched my stomach and closed my eyes. Sickness crept, and I waited to throw up. Aching bones throbbed and the burn in my stomach grew stronger. With each tick of the clock I waited for the end of this five-day treatment. And with each tick of the clock, the cure for my disease didn't seem to bring me closer, but rather further away from the fortunate life I lived before cancer.

Doctors and family members reassured me, speaking positively about the day when cancer would be forever behind me. Yet, they were on the outside of the needles and sickness, looking in, just as I'd felt while sitting in Bone Tumor Clinic only last Tuesday. The experts who cared for me, and the family who loved me, had no idea how discouraging it was to think about the "someday," when life would be cancer-free once again.

I could scarcely imagine the day when the treatment-after-treatment schedule that'd been adopted was forever behind me. A life without chemotherapy and medicine-cabinet-smelling hospital air seemed further than the promise of Christmas morning on the day when every ornament is taken from the tree.

I had few scars and none of the grown-up toughness that would build up in me hour after hour, day after day, thickening my skin and emotions. I stood foolish, tender, and soft in the midst of my first treatment, missing all the calluses I needed for this difficult journey.

Sickness peaked and so did my discouraging thoughts. *This is my life.* For as far as I could see into the future there was only sickness and cancer. When I looked at my grandmother to ask for a bucket, I noticed that her face wore other lines that weren't caused by smiles. Those lines were caused by worry and heartbreak, her father's suicide, the Great Depression, by the freight train that collided with her oldest son's 1966 Firebird, killing him instantly, and now sitting next to a grandson in a cancer ward.

I knew that neither the lines left from smiles nor the lines left from sadness appeared overnight, because I didn't have either. There'd been no shortcut leading Grandma past hard times or long smiles.

The doctors' advice rang in my ears: "day-to-day" and "step-by-step." I'd have no shortcut. Survival wasn't going to be easy. Waiting for my last treatment was going to be discouraging. Waiting for a miraculous toughness to appear and make treatment more bearable, would be discouraging. I could only wait for calluses to slowly form, day-to-day, and for each treatment to slowly end, step-by-step, as the second hand passed the lines on the clock's face.

Chapter Ten

Grateful Travis

Every hour in treatment was drawn out, but the nights were longest. The repetitions and side effects that came with chemo were the same night and day, but during the night they seemed worse. It's like those creaks and squeaks you hear all day long, but once the lights are switched off at bedtime, without warning the noises become creepy and loud; you pull the covers way up to your chin and are sure the boogieman is sneaking out of the closet or out from under the bed. In the same way, all the things that annoyed me during chemo during the day grew bigger when it was dark, distancing me from rest, stretching the night, attacking my body, and wearing down my patience.

My IV pole was equipped with a pump that pushed bags of chemo into my veins. IV bags full of saline followed every bag of chemotherapy, flushing the chemicals from my veins, and minimizing damage to my body. The pump was also equipped with an alarm that sounded with an authoritative "beep" for the nurses, telling them when one bag of fluid was emptied and another should be attached. The combination of drugs and constant dilution led to the sickness that I'd been feeling, the ache in my bones, a bladder busting at the seams, and an entire being that hated the *beep...beep... beep* of an IV pump.

I felt as if an invisible index finger repeatedly poked me, keeping rest at a distance. My aching bones throbbed almost constantly...poke...poke. Bags of fluid were pushed into my veins, forcing me to stand over a urinal every few minutes...poke... poke. The sickness kept its cycle, forcing my head into a bucket a few times an hour... poke...poke. Each of the three patients in my room had an IV pump, and each pump took turns beeping throughout the evening...poke...poke.

These pokes continued hour after hour during the night, and night after night during my treatment. A stream of dreamless, restless, sandpapered nights rubbed against me. The long nights irritated my days, making both more difficult. Finally, the night's extra unpleasantness completely took hold of the days, making every piece of every twenty-four hours equally tough. Even the break of morning, which had promised some relief toward the beginning of treatment, became as difficult as every other hour.

So far, I'd taken everything in stride, but in the darkness of one evening, near the end of my first treatment, the "pokes" pushed me too far. I'd arrived at a breaking point. I was about to run away, cry, or scream out—when I heard an unexpected sound. In the most tormented hour of my short battle with cancer, I heard something that shut down my silent complaining. Had my ear not picked up the sound, I would've continued on to the following moment, and surely cracked!

I heard a voice as constant as any other of the hospital's repetitions, but unlike the noisy beeps, stings, nausea, and stretching bladder, this sound was quiet: Travis spoke kindly to a nurse.

"Thank you," he said softly.

His words and tone sent my mind sailing back through the few days I'd spent with him in treatment. I took hold of each memory I had of Travis's voice. My thoughts of Travis started with the most recent. Grabbing upon the latest memory, I swung my mind astern. I thought back to the day I first met him.

Travis's voice was never irritated. He never asked why a nurse needed to poke him with a needle, why another prod by a doctor was necessary, or what exactly had been given to him on his meal tray. It didn't matter if Travis's IV bag was empty for the thousandth time, or the bag attached to the shunt draining fluid from around his brain tumor was full, nor the time of day or night. Travis's attitude was always the same. At any time, and in every instance, his voice was soft and full of gratitude. I wanted to be more like Travis.

I'd known Travis for less than a week. But we had spent almost all of my first five-day chemotherapy treatment together, and not once did I hear him complain. After every bathroom break or urinal trip, meal tray, or blood-pressure pump, Travis's response was always the same. "Thank you," he said politely. The sincerity of his gratitude won over the hospital staff taking care of him and warmed the bitter thoughts and feelings inside me.

Travis wasn't thanking the staff for poking or waking him. He was not happy to have a tumor or his life held by the thread of an IV and a hospital bed. He was thanking these people for helping him through his disease and treatment. Travis knew that needles held the power to sting, and the unending pump of liquids into his veins would disturb his night's sleep. However, the unpleasantness was only half of the story—Travis also knew that every sting from a needle and midnight wakeup brought him a step closer to health.

* * * * *

A Look Back: Without Lemons, There's no Lemonade

At age eleven, the stained-glass window of my healthy childhood was shattered; the beauty of unspoiled fun was broken by a threat, and my innocence and naiveté scattered as cancer pushed me to grow up. I learned about life, gained knowledge, and earned scars with each experience. The older I became, the more I understood the world's workings, and this caused wonder, both bright and gray, to fade.

Before cancer, I remember having a perspective of simplicity, an elementary understanding differentiating truth from lies, right from wrong. This understanding also faded as I got older, and the gray area between truth and falsehood, and right and wrong, broadened. But this gray area did not fill with any kind of wonder—instead it came with compromise and justification.

For me, the evening with Travis was a strong example of a type of childhood understanding. Now that I am older, I see Travis and what he taught me in a different light, but the simple truth I learned at age eleven has not changed. It took me many years to articulate this lesson, but from the instant I recognized Travis's voice and my lamentation halted, I knew. His calm and quiet voice spoke of revelation, and he made me realize something of circumstance.

I understood that there is always a little bad in every good day, and some good in the bad ones. My thoughts on that night had less to do with wanting to "make lemons into lemonade," and more to do with realizing that "without lemons there would be no lemonade." Every action by a doctor or nurse, and every reaction from the chemo, came about for one reason: to save me. All the unpleasantness I suffered on the receiving end of the needles provided the possibility for a cure. The more days I spent sick, the more I appreciated the health I had enjoyed all of my life. The more I was exposed to fears I never knew existed, the more I was forced to overcome those fears. On this night I understood a union between suffering and healing, sickness and health, courage and fear, a union that creates a constant waltz called "Everyday Life."

I did not have the chance to spend a great deal of time with Travis as I fought cancer, and we did not have the deep friendship that would develop between Chad, Erik, and me. Our friendship was brief, but because of Travis, I understood clearly and early in my fight through cancer that I could not choose many of the circumstances that would direct my life. But I could choose how I would react to those circumstances.

Chapter Eleven

McDonald House Breakfast Club

By the end of my first five-day treatment, passing time was marked less by dawn and dusk, and more by the steam and scent of coffee. A fresh cup of coffee marked the end of a shift sitting beside my bed for one family member and the beginning for another. Slowly, the shifts passed and my first treatment ended.

Chad and Travis were released a few fresh cups before me, and I was eager to follow. They hadn't traveled far; just over to the Ronald McDonald House, which was their home away from home. Erik, however, seemed stuck in his hospital bed. There didn't appear to be a specific number of days before he'd be released. It wasn't even a topic of conversation for Erik or his parents. I didn't understand their lack of excitement, because leaving was the only thought in my mind.

I could only compare the end of a harsh winter or the feel of a cool river on a hot August afternoon to leaving the hospital after a long, hard stay. My mind was fixed on the moment of release for days—being freed from sickness and given the chance to refresh. The end of this treatment meant a real bed, rest, and food. After my last bag of saline finished, and my IV pump beeped for the last time, it was all I could do not to jump up and run out the front doors of Children's Hospital. But as much as I wanted to, I could only move slowly.

By the end of the five days, even ordinary tasks required all the energy I could muster. Even lacing up my sneakers left me winded. I was asked if I needed a wheelchair or a nurse to escort me to our van, since, at most, I had only traveled a dozen or so steps in one direction over the past week.

"No, thanks," I said proudly, standing up and walking toward my freedom.

When I passed the bathroom I couldn't wait to be outside, to get some fresh air. Exiting our room I could almost feel a restful night's sleep, and about halfway to the elevator I could almost taste a cheeseburger. And that was as far as I got on my own. Weakness kept me from making it to the elevator.

A chemotherapy-fatigued body forced me to sit down in the hallway. I didn't fall or make a scene, but gently pressed my back against the wall and slowly slid to the floor. I sat on the tile floor drained of strength and breath. Just weeks earlier, I'd played on a basketball team; after my first treatment, I wasn't able to walk one court length.

A nurse appeared from around a corner with a wheelchair. She helped me off the tile and into the chair.

What a wimp, I thought.

"Thanks," I told her. Pride had vanished and I was genuinely grateful as she pushed me toward the elevators.

Just before we got there, Mom and Dad turned and went into another hospital room. The nurse followed them, guiding me through the doorway. I assumed it was Erik's room when my parents took the turn, and I was right. When I went in, I saw Rick and Sheri sitting beside his bed.

"I'll take it from here," I told the nurse.

I wheeled myself to the far side of Erik's bed.

"They're letting you out, Jason?" Erik asked.

"Yeah," I replied, trying to sound unenthused.

Erik's room was different than mine. He didn't have any roommates, there were posters and pictures on all the walls, and a big red couch sat near the foot of his bed. Erik hadn't been excited about being released from the hospital because he was settled in for a long stay. And in front of him, I didn't want to talk about the relief I felt about leaving. Erik, however, did want to talk about it.

Our parents also talked on the other side of the room. Their conversation became unimportant. It was just a buzz of chatter lost in the background as Erik described how good it feels not to be sick, to sleep through the night, and how delicious my first real meal outside the hospital was going to taste.

"What'll you eat first?" Erik asked.

"I've been dreaming about a cheeseburger."

Erik smiled, "Good choice."

"What about you, Erik? When're you gonna get outta here?"

The smile left Erik's face, he took a deep breath, and then he exhaled his answer.

"Pretty soon," he sighed.

His words, though soft, were confident. And though I asked the question, his answer wasn't truly directed at me. Erik's attention moved to the skyline outside the window by his bed. He stared into the distance, and neither of us said anything for a few moments.

"Shall we get you across the street, Jase?" my mother asked, reaching into our conversation from across the room.

Her words broke Erik from his thoughts, and he again smiled.

"I'll see you soon," he told me.

"See you soon," I replied.

It would seem that after lying around for a week in the hospital, I'd want to do something besides sleep, but I didn't. When we got to the McDonald House, I went straight to bed. There was a mountain of reasons why my bed at the McDonald House was better than my bed at the hospital. You could start with the lack of antiseptic smell, the *beep...beep...beeps*, the chemo, and from there I could keep going alphabetically from A to Z. Never mind the reasons, it was like heaven when I slipped my

McDonald House Breakfast Club

exhausted body into the cool cotton sheets.

By the next morning, the sickness had faded, and my muscles weren't as weak. Our room was empty, and I guessed that my family had gone to the kitchen for breakfast. By the time I reached the kitchen, any normal spectator would've thought that I'd just run a marathon. To catch my breath, I sat in the first available chair at the counter. Chad was sitting at the opposite end.

"You need to quit smoking, Jay," he joked.

I smiled and shook my head. I never knew what to say back to this kid. Catching my breath, I walked to Chad's end of the counter and sat next to him. I tried to think of a funny come-back for Chad, but Mom interrupted.

"I thought I heard you in here," Mom said, looking in around the kitchen door.

She put an arm around each of us and asked, "How're you boys feeling this morning?"

Chad straightened up his torso, threw both of his arms straight out to his sides, and then slowly curled each arm—flexing his biceps, "Strong!" he answered.

Mom shook her head. "And you, Jason, how're you feeling?"

"Still sick, I guess," I answered.

"Well, you should try and eat something...I'll make you my specialty," she said.

Mom's specialty was burnt toast, and nothing I'd ever done or said in the past allowed me to stay away from her cooking. I'd have to try and eat a little.

"Sounds good Mom."

Chad and I sat together and talked while we had breakfast. The only difference was, as I choked down small bits of burnt toast, Chad changed the IV bags connected to a small tube that poked from his stomach. Even so, there we sat—me with my toast and Chad with his feeding tube, having breakfast and talking.

We hadn't talked a whole lot in the hospital, and what conversations we did have were drug-affected and often cut short by throwing up. Chad made up for our lack of chitchat. He told me a million cancer war stories, about good nurses and bad food. He'd been fighting this disease for three years, and there was a story for every scar on his body. I think every one of his limbs had been opened with a scalpel.

"That's a lot of operations, Chad," I said.

"You're telling me," he replied. "But I'm still kicking."

Chad was a seasoned veteran when it came to chemotherapy and surgery; he even had some favorite scars from some favorite operations. He called the really good surgeries "double whammies."

"If you get lucky, Jay, they'll do two surgeries at the same time, only one hospital stay, only one anesthetic—a 'double whammy'!"

That morning, Chad told me more about his favorites, the stuff he really loved. He talked about his mother, brother, photography, radio-controlled cars, and the American machine named "Corvette."

"Since Make-A-Wish couldn't get me a real Corvette, I spent my wish soupin' up my RC car—that stands for radio-controlled car, Jay—with miniature Corvette parts," Chad said.

Make-A-Wish did him one even better. They'd picked Chad up in a limousine, driven him to a hobby shop, "souped-up" his RC car, and bought him the radio-controlled monster truck I'd seen in the hospital.

"Cancer's like flying through a dark cloud," he told me. "Once I get through the cloud, I see the rest of the sky. The blue sky's the rest of my life. Yeah, God's the plane, Mom's my copilot, and the cloud is only temporary. You know, Jay?"

"I think so," I answered.

"That's why I decided to spend my Make-A-Wish on a toy. I'll travel later, travel, and take pictures," he explained. "But right now I wanna try and be a kid."

Chad also told me about Tai-Kwan-Do.

"Yeah...I'm a black belt...no big deal," he said.

He told me about his home in Twisp, Washington, and about the cute girls in his high school. We must've sat there for hours talking, laughing, and having breakfast. Talking with Chad reminded me of finding a new favorite song on the radio, and I didn't want it to end. Unfortunately, Chad had to leave and go to the hospital.

Chad didn't want to go; it may've been the breakfast and conversation, or whatever dreaded treatment waited for him at the hospital. In any case, he thought that we should have breakfast again.

"Same time, same place, tomorrow, Jay?" he asked.

"I'll be here."

And so our "Breakfast Club" began. Every day Chad and I'd sit in the same seats, at pretty much the same time, and have breakfast, me with my toast, and Chad with his feeding tube.

Both Chad and I had several weeks of doctoring to do before we could return to our homes. The stretch left my family and his with time to spend in Seattle. Breakfast soon became a meeting spot to plan whatever we were going to talk our parents into doing on that particular day. Sometimes hospital visits and blood tests broke up our daily outings, but many times breakfast was the jumping-off point, leading us to sporting events or Seattle's wharf. Our favorite place to visit was a sports bar near the hospital. Chad and I ordered one meal of baby back ribs and one mud pie, then split them both down the middle.

After the weakness and sickness from my first five-day treatment wore off, I felt fine, and I had weeks before my next treatment. Chad, however, wasn't as fortunate. He was in and out of the hospital for radiation treatments almost every day. Because of the treatments, his stomach was a mess, and his primary nourishment came from his feeding tube. When Chad ate regular food, it was for the enjoyment of the outing and taste of the food.

An outing to the sports bar usually consisted of Chad excusing himself from the table two or three times so he could walk to the bathroom and throw up. At first this seemed strange, but it took me no more than a moment to get used to the routine. Chad returned from the bathroom, happily sat down at the table, and wasting no time, resumed eating.

* * * * *

A Look Back: Chad and Cherié

If a person spent much time at all with Chad and his mother Cherié, they'd ultimately see their similar spirits, humor—character. Character seldom arises with ease, and although their character was strengthened while facing cancer, it had developed through difficulties faced long before Chad's diagnosis.

Chad was born in Portland, Oregon, in 1975. Bill, his only brother, was four when Chad came along. Early on, it was clear that Cherié, Bill, and Chad were on their own. Cherié was a struggling single mother. She labored to financially provide for the boys, to be a loving mother, an authority figure, and a best friend. Still, Cherié made no apologies and never played the victim role. She emphasized love, personal faith, and a dependence on one another; this emphasis allowed the three of them not only to get by, but to be the kind of family that drew others to them.

When Bill grew older, he left for school and a job outside of Seattle. During his absence, as Chad remembered, "It was just Mom and me." As Chad got older and his character developed, the bond between mother and son became stronger. Cherié depended on Chad's sense of humor, personality, and attitude, none of which were ever discouraged.

When Chad was nine, he asked to take Tai-Kwan-Do, and the sport became his first love. Cherié loved Tai-Kwan-Do only because her boy loved the sport. Nobly, she shuffled schedules and shifts at work, getting Chad to Tai-Kwan-Do practice and tournaments. She rarely missed a tournament and always cheered loudly from the bleachers. Chad's Tai-Kwan-Do coach described her as "a yeller."

In 1988, when Chad was thirteen, he and Cherié moved to Twisp, Washington, and Chad became the first Junior Black Belt in the state. That same year, while at a Tai-Kwan-Do tournament, Chad was kicked in the leg and a bump developed on his muscle. The bump would not go away and was later diagnosed as cancer.

Chad took much of his Tai-Kwan-Do mentality into his fight through cancer. Disciplined and focused, he brought the mind-over-matter attitude he once used to break boards and win tournaments, into his treatment. He was a fighter, and like his mother he made no apologies and never played the victim role.

Three years after Chad's diagnosis, I was wheeled into his room at Children's Hospital. Cherié and Chad closed the curtain surrounding his bed, giving them as much privacy as was available in the hospital room. Cancer had killed too many of Chad's friends. He and his mother had been involved in the lives of too many families facing the disease and they could not carry another. They hid behind the curtain until my grandfather, uninvited, stuck his head into their space.

"Where's this boy's father?" Harp grumbled with the social tact of a wild elephant.

Chad and Cherié sat surprised, looking at my grandfather. *What do you care?* Cherié thought. She was not the type of person to let a comment like my grandfather's go without reply. She poised herself to say something sarcastic that would shut Harp up and get him out of their personal space. However, for reasons that Cherié still cannot explain, she answered politely.

"Well, obviously, he's not around much," Cherié said, still hoping that Harp would leave them alone.

He stayed where he stood, and my grandfather's comment, as Cherié says, "began a conversation with my family that would never end."

* * * * *

The first months I spent in Seattle weren't easy. Fortunately, Chad was living there nearly all of that time. He was sixteen, a few years older than me, but we were the same height, width, even almost the same weight. And if you found one of us, the other wasn't far behind.

I know it sounds strange, but those first months had more laughter in them than any other time I could remember. I don't think a day passed when Chad and I didn't find ourselves laughing about something. Sometimes it seemed that the harder the day was, the more there was to laugh about.

Believe me—once you step into the world of cancer, many things that were important before then suddenly weren't worth worrying about. That made room for paying attention to the things that really mattered, like enjoying—right now—the moment you're in. Noticing those small gifts, so often overlooked, stirred up smiles and laughter when a smile or a laugh seemed impossible.

Like when Harp stumbled over a shoe on the floor at Children's and knocked a picture off the wall, leaving a knot on his head the size of Pluto. Or when Dad farted much louder than expected while we were at a movie. Or, when Mom was combating Seattle traffic on the way to an MRI scan and backed over a fire hydrant with the minivan. Then there was the time Chad and I bought disappearing ink from a magic shop at Pike's Place Market and sprayed a non-suspecting intern doctor from a whole different country. "Well guess dis' is America," he said in an Indian accent, just after we covered his neatly pressed white shirt with blue ink. The best one though, was when Chad snuck a goldfish into a hospital urinal. Chemotherapy was so strong that even after washing all the pee out of the container, the fish only lasted a few minutes—it didn't matter, we laughed until we cried when a nurse found that dead fish.

Maybe laughing was the only thing to do. Maybe we all would have gone nuts without squeezing some humor out, wherever we could. I'm not sure how, but along with new sickness, scariness, and stress in life, there were also new reasons to laugh. Comedy crept into my days through my father, grandfather, grandmother, mother, and brother, but Chad's jokes, actions, and reactions made me laugh more than anything or anyone. Chad was hilarious. His personality mixing with other kids at Children's and the McDonald House was always funny. Chad's personality mixing with my brother's good nature and stubbornness, made for the best laughs.

Chad, my brother, and I were together all the time. If any one of us was unhappy with one or the other, we let it be known. Chad especially; he'd let anybody, anywhere know what was on his mind, and one afternoon Jon learned his lesson.

Jon leaned in with a tissue, "You got a little something in your nose," he said to Chad, quietly, trying not to embarrass him.

Chad pulled away and looked at Jon with a sharp eye.

"It's not a booger, it's snot," he replied shaking his head, deliberately making, "It's not" and "it's snot" impossible to tell apart.

As if he were telling a secret, Jon again spoke softly, "You got a little—"

"It's snot." Chad said louder. "You think it's a booger, but it's snot," he said shaking his head.

"It's not?" Jon asked confused.

"No. It's snot, Jon. Get it? It's snot! It's snot!" Chad barked.

"Okay, okay," Jon answered, "It's not...gee whiz. I'm just trying to help."

"Well, it's not a booger, it's just snot," Chad concluded matter-of-factly, as if the two were coming to an agreement.

"It's not, Chad," Jon replied, still puzzled. "But, what is it then?"

"Snot," Chad answered, "Can I have the Kleenex please?"

Jon handed him the tissue, which he had completely forgotten was in his hand.

"Or maybe a booger," Chad continued, blowing his nose.

Jon got it, "Hey," he griped.

Jon wanted to protest being made fun of but it was hard to keep up with Chad's wit. Instead of trying, Jon thought that he'd give Chad a couple of slugs in the arm and throw him into a headlock. Chad was in no mood for a headlock.

"Jon, seriously, I've been sick all morning. Quit screwing around." My brother's arm muffled his voice.

My brother thought he was being funny and kept roughhousing. After all, Chad was just skin and removed bones, tubes and detached muscles. *What could he do to a bigger and hairier Jon, anyway?*

"Thanks for the tissue. I'm sorry for picking on you. But if you don't let me go I'm gonna get mad."

After the final warning, when Jon didn't quit, Chad's toothpick arms shot into action.

"You're gonna get it now," he grunted.

In the time it took me to blink, Chad was out of the headlock. He gave my brother a Tai-Kwan-Do shot to the sternum like it was nothing. Then, in the same second, eighty-five pounds of Chad somehow flipped one hundred and sixty pounds of Jon flat on his back. Jon got up in a hurry, trying to dodge embarrassment, but you can bet he didn't have any more thoughts of roughhousing on his mind. More like shock.

Chad's words and actions always seemed to be timed, patient, exact, and wise. Whether Chad threw out a joke or knocked somebody on their rear end, I looked up to him more every single day.

It hit me that I should've carried a notepad during those mornings and outings, because Chad was like a professor. He was an expert in tough times and their bright sides. His wisdom and unique point of view didn't come in spite of critical times, but because of them. Chad could offer up a joke and a smile when either seemed impossible, because he'd already overcome almost everything that could get in a person's way.

Chad could enjoy the taste of good food, savor good times with his family and friends, because he'd gone without. Three years of fighting for his life had left him with the ability to enjoy the moment he was in, and notice tiny things that others so often took for granted. My friend was a pro at pointing out life's most overlookable gifts—even the correct way to throw up.

Chapter Twelve

Bald by Eleven

Cancer was everywhere. There was no moment, thought, idea, ache or pain, burst of energy or breathless moment that didn't change, or wasn't changed by my cancer—there was always a piece of it with me, somewhere, in something.

Even days spent outside the hospital were filled with thoughts of test results, treatments, and surgeries, those that'd ended, and those still coming up. My mind and my family's minds were cluttered by cancer thoughts. Always in either the front, or the back of my mind, cancer stole much of my energy and life became exhausting. Fortunately, Chad had a defense against getting tired.

"You just don't slow down until you're ready for bed, Jay," he told me more than once.

So that's what we did. Chad and I ran until we were completely exhausted. Assuming doctor schedules allowed, we started our day at breakfast, and refused to slow down until we split ways at bedtime. Actually, when we felt good, our favorite pastime was eating: breakfast, snacks, lunch, snacks, dinner, dessert, snacks. We usually split or sampled, never big portions, it was taste we were after, because a week of cold cereal, Kool-Aid, and puking was always just around the corner. We tried to get the most out of every day spent outside the hospital, though most days finished on the second floor of Children's because Chad looked forward to visiting Erik.

Chad and Erik were close friends. They'd been treated at Children's together for about a year and were both in high school. I think the differences between the two were good for their friendship. Erik was soft-spoken, pale, and very tall, and he did most of the listening. Chad, well, he did most of the talking, was short, and his darker skin made him look healthier than the rest of us. Even with Erik, Chad was the veteran, I think he might've been Children's longest-standing patient.

I was younger and new to cancer. I knew nothing compared to the two of them, but Chad and Erik passed on bits of advice, keeping me included in their talks.

"Take the Mesna home, it can get you out of the hospital sooner," Erik told me about a drug we were given to minimize chemotherapy side-effects.

"At home?" I asked.

"Yeah, Jay, it doesn't have to be through an IV. You can drink it," Chad said. "It'll shave off at least five hours of hospital time."

"It's gross, though, tastes like the inside of a bicycle tire," Erik added.

"Don't ask, Jay," Chad said. "Go smell the inside of a bike tire, and that's what Mesna tastes like…it's like rubbery or something…I swear."

I was beginning to feel left out. Not because of Chad's and Erik's knowledge or their friendship, but because I had a full head of hair. My friends, as well as many other children at the hospital or Ronald McDonald House, were bald. It'd been weeks since I was released from my first treatment, and not a single hair had left my head. *What's going on?* I wondered.

After leaving Erik's room, I asked Chad, "Why do you think I still have my hair?"

"Some kids never lose their hair," he said, like it was an obvious answer.

To say the least I was disappointed. *I mean, all that work: exhaustion, throwing up, falling down, peeing every seven seconds, and I was going to be the oddball, the one kid with a full head of hair.*

By the time we got back to the McDonald House, I had so much anxiety about not going bald that I burst into a line of questions. I asked Chad questions until my face turned blue.

"Is my hair gonna fall out?"

"If it does, will I have a nice-shaped head like yours?"

"Will it be shiny like yours?"

"Will my head look tan like yours?"

Chad stopped my inquisition.

"Alright," he interrupted, "come on!"

He rolled his eyes, grabbed my sleeve, and guided me to one of the McDonald House's common bathrooms. He sat me down on the toilet.

"Welcome to my office," he said.

He pulled his glasses from his front shirt pocket and placed them on the tip of his nose.

He gave me a stern look and said, "You need to stop dreaming of a tan head right now, Jay. Maybe one summer day your freckles will connect, but you just don't have the genes to look this good!"

He had the ability to piss me off and make me laugh all at the same time.

Chad's face was still stern, and he tilted his head back to look down the slope of his nose through his glasses. Resembling an old doctor, he examined my scalp. He took hold of the hair on my head and began moving tufts so he could see beneath. Pulling handfuls of my hair from side to side, he attentively looked at every part of my scalp. He examined my head from front to back, and when finished, he came to a conclusion.

"In my professional opinion, your head's nicely shaped," he announced.

I was glad to have a nice shaped-head, and that the somewhat painful scalp examination was over. However, he wasn't finished. He pulled my hair one more time just for fun.

"Hey!" I protested.

His last tug felt different. It didn't sting or even feel like someone had pulled my hair. But the surprised look on Chad's face made me wonder if he'd popped the lid right off the front of my head.

Bald by Eleven

Chad looked at his clenched fist, his eyes widened and his mouth opened. Then, as suddenly as it had appeared, his look of surprise vanished, and his grin returned. He spoke to me with worry in his voice, that you knew right away was fake.

"Jay...look!" he said sarcastically.

Chad opened his fist, showing me a clump of brown hair. We both knew that the hair didn't come from Chad. It was mine. There was genuine worry on my face and in my voice, when I asked, "What'd you do?"

Chad grinned. I soon smiled too, realizing I was finally going to fit in.

He placed his smiling face in his hands, and again filled his voice with sarcasm.

"What're you going to complain about now, Jay?" he asked, "You've a nice-shaped head, and now you get to show it off."

Sitting there on the toilet, the day caught up with me. Going bald took my last bits of energy. Without warning, I was completely exhausted and if Chad hadn't been there I might've leaned my head against the toilet paper roll and taken a short nap.

"See, you slowed down, sat in one place too long," Chad said.

"Guess so," I replied

"Well...see you at breakfast, old buddy," he said, leaving the bathroom.

"See you tomorrow at breakfast, Chad," I replied.

Leaving the bathroom, I walked directly to my room at the McDonald House and, fast as ever, I fell asleep. More of my hair fell out during the night, but I slept so deeply that I had no idea, and by morning I was laying on a pile of brown hair. When I woke, it was to a mouth full of curls and a panicked mother. I'd fallen asleep so quickly the night before that I'd forgotten to tell my parents the exciting news.

New to the world of cancer, both of my parents were on emotional overload, teetering on the edge of totally stressing out. Seeing my half-bald head for the first time tipped the scale in the wrong direction, and pushed Mom over the top. She was in a panic.

Poor Mom was about to cry as she tried to get a doctor on the phone. Maybe she didn't expect my hair to fall out so soon, or all at once. Maybe the night's sleep clouded her thoughts and she had slipped back into the routine of our old life, back to a time, not so long ago, when a bald eleven-year-old should really worry his parents.

I watched as Mom found out the hard way that her neck was more elastic than the phone cord. As she talked, she paced one direction, forgot that the phone was attached to a cord that was attached to the wall, and walked a few steps too far. The cord stopped Mom with a jerk that nearly knocked her down, but then she regained her footing, reversed, and paced to the other end of the room. On her way, Mom again forgot that she was holding a phone—with a cord—attached to the wall. And again her head and neck took the brunt of the backward jerk.

Mom's voice rose to the point of noise pollution. She probably didn't even need the telephone. I believe that the nurse on the other end could hear her voice bellowing from the McDonald House, across the street, and into the hospital.

Dad's morning had started a few moments after mine, but just as abruptly. When the hollering began, he'd jumped out of bed. It was funny to see Dad, now affectionately referred to by Chad as "The Old Reverend," following my mother around the room in his boxer shorts. Being a good husband, it was his duty to stand by Mom and support her, yet he had no idea what he was supporting her in. My father desperately wanted to know why my mother was screaming into the phone receiver, pacing back and forth, and voluntarily giving herself whiplash.

Thankfully, I'd figured out what was going on before him.

"Guys…"

"Guys!"

"GUYS!" I finally yelled.

Both of my parents stared at me, looking like deer caught in the headlights of our minivan.

"Whoooaaa there, everything is aaaaaaalright," I cautioned, both palms up as if I were calming a herd.

"Dad," I said, lifting my arm, pointing to an unevenly bald head—unnatural, ugly, and far from the clean, smooth scalps of Chad and Erik.

Suddenly Dad understood why Mom was screaming.

Turning to my mother, still pointing at my head, I said, "Remember, Mom. Around here, it's weird to *have* hair."

Mom stopped hyperventilating.

"Chad pulled the first bunch out last night…must've kept falling out while I was sleeping."

"Son," Dad said calmly, "you need a haircut."

Mom hung up the phone. She turned her head slowly from side to side and rubbed the back of her neck. I slumped into my bed with a sigh. Dad put on his jeans and went into the hall. He explained the noise pollution to a crowd of concerned people now gathered outside our door.

"She'll recover in no time," the Old Reverend reassured.

And Jon, my caring brother, snored loudly, sleeping soundly through the whole thing.

* * * * *

A Look Back: Siblings Left Alone

It would be difficult to find two more different people than Jon and me. Jon was big and stocky; he was patient and forgiving. I was skinny, could hold a grudge, and had a temper that, when lit properly, popped like a firecracker.

My brother was one who immersed himself in the process: tying the fly and casting the line, making his bicycle shine before pedaling, and knowing well the characters and plot of a book he might be reading. I would just as soon use a fishing net, ride my bike until a wheel fell off, and read only the last page of a story. We were dissimilar and clashed more times than brothers should while growing up.

My older brother regarded cancer as a disease old people had, and from which they subsequently died. He had trouble grasping how children could have cancer, and this put Jon a step behind understanding my disease and the changes in our family's life.

Jon believed I was too ornery to allow anyone or anything to beat me. He hated being at the hospital, the smell and the sounds, watching me vomit and my mother cry. He could see my struggle and discomfort, but there was no doubt in his mind that my fight through cancer would be won and life would return to normal.

Although constantly surrounded by people, in different ways my brother and I were each alone throughout my cancer. Any bump or bruise on either one of us was confronted aggressively with thorough testing because our parents automatically assumed the worst. Along with Jon's hatred for the hospital, the overreaction by our parents caused Jon to bite his lip and keep any troubles to himself.

"Just leave me alone," was a phrase, barbed on purpose, that my brother frequently used to keep melodrama and real drama away from him.

Jon withdrew from the hospital and shut down his emotions as much as he could; he read or watched movies, seizing any available moment away from our family. Becoming independent, he began to grow up quicker than most of his peers.

In many ways my brother was the strongest and wisest of us all. Jon could see that he was on the outside of the needles and the chemo. While others scrambled to be in the center of something they did not understand Jon looked from afar. He believed that if a person was not going through treatment themselves, they could not relate, and he was glad I found good friends who truly understood what cancer felt like.

Jon watched the growing friendship between Chad, Erik, and me, and he knew it was our difficulty that drew us close. Oftentimes, he accompanied Chad and me as we visited Erik, content to quietly sit alongside the three of us. Although he was in our company, he kept my friends at a distance, wanting the experience of cancer and treatment to finish as quickly as possible.

Chad, however, did allow Jon the privilege of driving his precious Radio-Controlled Monster Truck that he received for his Make-A-Wish, a privilege that was not even given to his own mother. Unfortunately, the first time Jon drove the miniature truck, he accidentally crashed it into Chad's ankle. Then, as Jon was busy apologizing to Chad, he lost track of the Monster Truck and weaved it in between the tires of a moving bus. Once Chad regained command of the controller and guided the truck to safety, he looked at my brother and shook his head.

"I don't even know what to say to you, Jon," Chad mumbled.

Chad never let my brother drive the Radio-Controlled Truck again. Jon did not begrudge Chad this decision. In fact, my brother must have had a good laugh later when no one else was around, because this incident is Jon's fondest memory of chemo and treatment, Children's Hospital, and Seattle.

Even as Jon drew further away from my family and me during cancer, he still sat beside my hospital bed, emptied dozens of urinals, and held his share of puke buckets. Nonetheless, we drifted apart at this time, and our closeness would not return until years later when Jon left for college. He regarded the split as natural; he desired independence and I needed care. Circumstance led us differently, and each of us responded and became strong in his own way.

Chapter Thirteen

The Chemo Cut

We couldn't find a barber shop as hard as we tried. We just kept running into the same beauty salon, and there was no way I was going to a beauty salon. At least, that's what I thought. But Mom had the ability, as mothers do, to talk her children into the unthinkable. Although I wasn't happy about it, we were soon walking inside that stupid salon.

Typically, the shop was long and narrow, mirrors the length of each wall. It smelled like perfume and was full of old women in curlers who I figured must all be somebody's grandmas. There were seats for haircuts, sinks for hair washing, and those weird chairs with the bubble lids that resemble astronaut helmets.

Get me outta here.

When we walked in the door, a middle-aged lady approached us. She had short red hair and a raspy voice. Without wavering she said something unusual.

"Looks like you need a Chemo-Cut."

I didn't know what to say. My head was covered by a baseball cap, so I had no idea how she knew what kind of haircut I needed.

The woman's remark had the opposite effect on my mother. Mom jumped into conversation, and a few minutes later the entire salon had heard my life's history, from birth to diagnosis.

Would you shut up, Mom, I thought, *can't we just get the haircut and get the heck out of here?*

A biography sounds odd in this situation, but I was beginning to get used to it. Lately Mom had been telling all kinds of unfamiliar people about my disease. She didn't get the hint that when a waitress asked, "How're you doing today?" the question didn't really need an in-depth answer.

People all over Seattle had started talking to Mom and gotten more than they bargained for. Waitresses, pizza delivery guys, receptionists, and other regular people crossing Mom's path learned all about my life and my cancer.

The hairdresser wasn't as confused as the other strangers. She listened carefully, and at some points in the story her eyes even welled with tears. When Mom finished, the hair dresser put her arm around me and walked me to an empty chair.

Running her fingers through her short red hair, she said, "I just got rid of my own Chemo-Cut."

My story had hit close to home. It had taken a lung transplant and a year of chemotherapy for her to stop smoking, but she broke the habit.

We chatted as she cut my hair—about the weather, what grade I was in, where we were from. A Chemo-Cut is really just a buzz cut, and she was done before I knew it. She used electric clippers to get my hair as close to the scalp as she could, but it wasn't close enough. The spots where the hair had actually fallen out still looked different than those that'd been buzzed.

Chemotherapy actually kills hair follicles, so in the places where my hair had fallen out, my scalp looked clean-shaven. In those spots there was no stub, whisker, or any other evidence of hair. On the other parts of my head, those buzzed by the electric razor, you could still see a flicker of hair.

In short, my head looked like an old piece of shag carpet with scattered pieces of shag missing. I looked stupid, but knew that it wouldn't be long before the rest of my hair would fall out.

"That's it?" I asked, relieved the haircut didn't take long.

"That's it," she answered proudly.

Rubbing my head and looking in the long mirror hanging on the wall in front of me, "Thanks for making me look…ummm…normal-*er*," I said.

"Come back and see me when your hair grows back," she said.

When we returned to the McDonald House, I found Chad at a table in the kitchen, eating Cheetos with Travis. I was wearing my hat.

"Hey guys," I said as I sat down.

Without taking his eyes off Travis, Chad sounded disinterested as he said, "Let's see it."

"No way!" I replied.

Chad looked at me, and asked again, "Come on, Jay…I'll see your head sooner or later," he said.

I refused, and tried to change the subject, "So what'd you guys do today?"

Chad didn't give up.

"Not a chance, Jay," he said. "Let's see it!"

He pestered me until I gave in. I took off my hat for a second or two. Then I quickly put it back on, took a Cheeto out of Chad's bag, and leaned back in my seat.

"There, you happy now?" I asked.

"Ha!" Chad laughed out loud.

He then shot a sharp, "No way!" toward Travis, who was reaching for his bag of Cheetos.

It didn't take a genius to figure out Chad was joking with Travis.

"Look Travis," Chad explained, "these Cheetos are the only food I can keep down right now. This bag is a special bag with pharmo-preservatives that help my nausea."

"Well, don't you think you could share just one…see if it helps with my nausea," Travis asked, in his soft-spoken, polite way.

Chad and I weren't exactly sure if chemo affected Travis's stomach the same way it did ours. He even finished the hospital meals that we joked about so often—down

The Chemo Cut

to the last bite. The only people I'd ever seen completely finish a meal at Children's were Travis and Grandpa Harp (who, coincidentally, shared a similar physique). All the same, Travis was asking a reasonable question, from one cancer kid to another.

"I don't know, man. This bag is doctor-prescribed specifically for me," Chad answered.

"Really?" Travis asked.

"No, not really," Chad said smiling, spinning the open end of the bag toward Travis. "These're normal Cheetos from a normal store. Have as many as you want. But they're one of the only things I can keep down these days, so you should ask next time before digging in."

Chad had busted Travis sneaking some of his Cheetos. He'd been caught "red-handed," Chad later explained. Taking someone's personal food was against the rules at the McDonald House, big time. As was Chad's way, rather than getting mad, he drew a joke from the situation, made it fun, and played his role as a kind of big brother at the house.

Chad and I sat at the table with Travis for while. We didn't talk much, both of us entertained by the obvious joy Travis got from simply snacking on Cheetos. We probably would've stayed there a long time, but suddenly Chad lost all the color in his face and slowly stood up.

"Hey, man, I gotta go," he said.

Pale, holding his stomach—his next stop was the bathroom.

Unfortunately, sickness was a familiar thing at the house. Travis and I paid little attention to Chad leaving. I figured that he was headed to the common bathroom just down the hall from the McDonald House's kitchen, and he'd be back at the table soon.

But when Chad came back, he drew the attention of the entire room. Furious, he stepped into the doorway with his fists clinched and placed on his hips. He loudly cleared his throat, and demanded to know, "Who was the person responsible for peeing on the toilet seat in the bathroom?"

If Chad was joking now, he sure fooled me. I was afraid for the guilty party.

A meek and shaky hand slowly rose from across my table. It'd have to be the most honest kid in the room, probably the only kid who would've admitted to peeing on the seat of a common toilet. Travis raised his hand and apologized for his mistake.

"I did. Sorry, Chad," he said.

"Travis, first the Cheetos and now this," Chad started tapping his foot, "Do you know what it's like to try and throw up in a toilet with someone else's pee on the seat?"

Travis thought for a moment, and then replied, "Don't think so?"

I wondered if we'd see a repeat of the same Tai-Kwan-Do skills Chad used on my brother.

This, of course, wasn't the case. "Would you mind cleaning the pee off the toilet seat?" Chad asked politely.

Chad put his arm around Travis, and I followed them as they walked down the hall and into the bathroom. Chad looked over Travis's shoulder while he cleaned off the seat.

"Thanks, man," Chad said, stepping out of the way so Travis could leave the bathroom.

"You're welcome," Travis answered softly, not phased one bit by the "doctor-prescribed" bag of Cheetos, peeing on the toilet seat, or cleaning off the seat.

Chad shook his head and then matter-of-factly shut the door, probably to finish the job that had been so rudely interrupted by some misguided dribbles.

Chapter Fourteen

Memories of Home

"Step-by-step" and "day-to-day" were clichés used nearly every day by someone around me, and were usually made true by some surprise, doing, or undoing. The constant in cancer treatment was change, and the only way to settle in was to bend, to bow, and to turn the corners it asked. My family and I had settled in to living in the midst of change, living in the short term. Planning beyond a day was risky, but in some cases we needed more than a moment's notice in order to make future plans. In these cases, we did everything we could to avoid surprises that might get in the way of, say, a baseball game.

Children's had three tickets to a big game for the Seattle Mariners, and I got them at a doctor's appointment between my first and second chemo treatments. The seats were behind the Mariners' dugout, and if that wasn't enough, I might even be able to go into the locker room after the game to meet the players. I was excited, but the game was during the coming weekend, a few long days away.

The tickets came at a great time. A little excitement was exactly what I needed. Not the "I just found out that I have cancer," or "I just began a new and slightly more nauseating kind of life" sort of excitement, but the "roasted peanuts, hot dog, giant soda, root...root...root for home team" kind of excitement.

I was looking forward to the game more than ever, because the McDonald House was more empty than usual. My brother needed to get back to school, and since Mom, Dad and I were settled in, used to the new routine of no routine, Grandma Dorie and Grandpa Harp took Jon home to Montana. After my brother and grandparents left, the house quieted even further when, on the next day, Chad and Cherié also left for a short trip home.

Chad had a break between chemo and radiation treatments. Doctors cleared him to leave, and he wanted to go home for a few days, sleep in his own bed, and see his friends. Lucky for him, Twisp, Washington, is closer to Seattle than Missoula, Montana.

As the baseball game got closer, I got more excited. On the night before the game, my excitement hit the sky—then came falling down. I woke up in the middle of the night shivering. I wrapped up as tightly as I could in my blanket, but chills still ran up and down my spine. It was a fever.

Mom took my temperature every few minutes for about a half-hour, but the mercury wouldn't fall. It was over a hundred degrees. Those five days of chemotherapy had not only destroyed cancer cells, but also killed all dividing cells. My white blood cell count had dropped and my immune system was weakened. Since I'd received the baseball tickets, I'd done whatever possible to avoid germs. I wore a surgical mask around anyone who thought they might have a cold, constantly washed my hands, stopped using drinking fountains, and even poured soda out of the can and into a glass. When my fever appeared, I knew it had all failed.

There are many reasons why a fever might crop up. They aren't all terrible, but for a body like mine, with a damaged immune system, they're especially dangerous. When a cancer patient has a fever, they go to the hospital right away, no matter what time it is. No matter what's planned the next day. So in the middle of the night, my parents and I went to the Emergency Room.

In my mind, the worst thing that could happen was a doctor admitting me to the hospital, which would result in three empty seats behind the Mariners' dugout. But that wasn't the worst possible result. I could have a widespread infection, so bad that they'd have to isolate me from everyone, including Mom and Dad. I could have an infection in my Port, which would mean another operation. And then there was the threat that patients and parents only whisper about, the worst kind of infections, which strike an immune system at its weakest, and you just plain die.

Because kids who have their hearts set on something usually can't see past that and on to the bigger picture, I prayed with all my might for the doctors not to admit me into the hospital. And, since mothers usually overreact, and cannot see past the worst-case scenario and on to the bigger picture, Mom prayed with all her might for the doctors to admit me to the hospital and do whatever it took to keep me alive. I guess God came to a compromise—I didn't die and could watch the game on the television from my hospital bed.

The infection was serious enough that they admitted me into the hospital, and all my hopes of going to the game were crushed. They accessed my Port and hooked me up to an IV pump. Antibiotics fought the infection, and ice cream helped my disappointment.

While in the hospital this time, everyone around me had to wear a surgical mask because I was so susceptible to germs. I couldn't even be in a room with other patients and their visitors. They gave me a single room all to myself that I called my "Suite." But this bit of good news came with a catch: no one would be able to stay in the room with me overnight.

I'd never been alone in the hospital. Mom had spent almost every night on the hide-a-bed next to my hospital bed. When she didn't stay, Dad or Grandma Dorie did. On this night, because of my low blood counts, the risk of a surgical mask slipping off one of their faces or of one of them coughing in my direction was too great.

The idea of staying alone scared me; although, I think it was even harder for Mom. Neither one of my parents wanted to stay across the street at the Ronald McDonald House, but both made the best of it. They did what they could to make me as comfortable as possible. My mother tucked me in, and my father read from the gospels. They put me at ease, and by the time they left, I didn't think I'd mind being

Memories of Home

by myself. But once the door closed behind them, I realized I was really alone. The room was quiet, the night hollowed, and I was lonely.

This time, the night didn't make things seem louder or more annoying. There were no creepy, boogieman kind of sounds. Around me the hospital wasn't totally silent, but all noise was distanced, filtered by the door to my Suite. I heard every closing door, brushing breeze, far-off beep, and muffled voice. But they were soft, far from anything bothersome, and far from anything that'd keep me from resting.

This stay was different than my previous stays in a hospital. I would've loved this quiet night, with no pain or vomit, following my shoulder surgery or my five-day chemo treatment. I'd wished for this then, for a deep and restful sleep. Now that it was possible, I wasn't tired. I was alone in the dark, unable to sleep, and overrun by my thoughts. There was only me, and only memory. My thoughts had an open range. My mind began to race. And when my mind raced, it often ran home.

Lying in my hospital bed, looking out the window into the darkness, I remembered barbecues and birthdays, family and friends, my grade school, and our house. The quiet night let loose thoughts filled with "remember whens." Scenes of merry and mischief were projected onto the window's glass, one after another. August swims would fall to November Thanksgivings, and winter snowmen would spring to summer evenings.

Remembering mornings when I could ride to school on my bike, I missed the hassle of setting the alarm a half-hour early for the extra time I needed to get my bike lock, fill my pack, and ride to school. The joy of speeding away from school at three o'clock, and sometimes not needing to check in at home until dinner, was a reward I waited for all winter.

I recalled the tricks I played on my brother during camping trips: taking the tent stakes out of the ground while Jon was sleeping, or filling his sleeping bag with pinecones before bed. In the mornings I stole Jon's fishing line and flies, replacing them with a can of earthworms, and then watched his frustration in the afternoon because he couldn't catch a thing.

I thought of catching frogs, turtles, and snakes by the river near my house, then forgetting about my slimy finds in the pockets of torn blue jeans, which Mom discovered on laundry day. I missed my Montana, and the endless energy that allowed me to do all these things.

These memories brought up a hollow, lonely feeling from within me. The night wasn't hollow just because the hospital was quiet, and I wasn't lonely just because this was the first night I'd spent alone. I had begun to really consider the "then and there," and the "here and now." The days back *then*—*there* in Montana, were so warm and full, and all the sickness *here, now* in the hospital seemed empty—I was really lonesome for the life we'd left behind.

"It'll all still be there when you get home," I heard a voice say.

Startled, I jerked toward the voice. This wasn't a voice from the past. Someone stood in my room, blanketed in the shadow of the doorway. From the silhouette, I could see this was a woman, a nurse. The outline showed her sturdy frame and short curly hair. Her voice was soft, quiet like the hospital around her, and brought me back to the evening at hand. As the nurse came closer, I recognized her face from my first treatment.

"What will?" I asked.

"Everything out those windows."

I wondered how she knew what I was thinking. Of course, I later understood that she didn't. It was a good bet that if a boy was lying on a bed in a hospital gazing out a window, he was probably thinking of something besides being sick.

"My name's Dianne," she said, "Do you remember me?"

I nodded.

I guess Dianne saw my parents while she was on her break. They asked her to come up to my room and check on me. She'd made my family feel comfortable during the previous chemo treatment. Her humor made it easy to get to know her. I remembered her jokes and her drinking huckleberry milkshakes with Harp. During the misery of that treatment, I didn't care about her jokes, or favorite flavor of milkshake. However, on this lonely evening she was just the person to put me at ease.

Dianne stayed and talked to me about my home and memories, about the many things I thought of while looking out the hospital window. After listening and listening, she offered good news.

"The beginning of treatment's always the worst and always seems the longest," Diane said.

"Think so?" I asked.

"Yes, I do, you'll have a couple treatments behind you, and be home for a visit before you know it," she answered.

I was glad that Diane spent her break with me.

"I have to go back to work," she said. "I'll check on you again later."

That night was different than others I'd spent in a hospital. There was no sickness or pain, no family, no Chad, and I deeply missed the fortunate life I lived and had taken for granted, as never before. But similar to other occasions of being lost in memories, I was interrupted. Diane sat with me, talked with me, and made the thought of going home, if only for a visit, feel not at all far off. Thinking of actually going home slowed my thoughts way down, and the night felt less lonely. Finally, I closed my eyes, believing that the many things I loved and missed *then*, were still waiting for me, *there*.

Chapter Fifteen

The Cancer Patient's Guide to Duct Tape

Having my own room and not hurting or feeling sick was pleasant, but like the five-day chemo treatment, time passed slowly. I should've been eating barbecued ribs and mud pie, enjoying the city, making the most of the time before my next treatment. But four white walls, an IV pole, and an infection kept me caged.

Dad came up with an idea that'd keep my eyes from following the hands of the clock. His idea was inspired by the trail of hair that followed me everywhere I went. My scalp was spotted with areas that still had hair and others that were smooth and bald. I constantly shed hairs left from the buzz cut, and if something wasn't done soon, someone would need to follow me around with a vacuum cleaner.

After leaving the room for an hour or so, Dad returned with a straight-edge razor and a bottle of shaving cream. These items helped solve a couple of problems: the razor could shave my head down to the scalp and stop my shedding, and also cure my boredom for a while.

Applying a steel blade to my scalp when my blood counts were low wasn't smart. Even a small nick could bring on another infection, keeping me caged and bored for a much longer amount of time. Dad wasn't worried; he'd been shaving for years. His skilled hands left me with an un-nicked, hairless head, well, almost hairless. The problem had gotten better, but wasn't yet solved. My head no longer looked like a worn out piece of carpet, and I wasn't shedding, but there was still some hair on my head: stubble.

Again, some spots were smooth, with no evidence of hair, because the follicle was dead, but in the other places there were tiny slivers of hair. The slivers could barely be seen, but I felt them every time I placed a hat on my head, or my head on a pillow. These dead hairs were trying to work their way out of my scalp. As they left, they caused a feeling of pins and needles when anything touched my skin.

It didn't take long for my father to come up with a solution to this problem as well. Since the hairs poked me as they fell out, Dad thought they just needed some help with their exit. The solution he came up with shouldn't have surprised me, but it did.

Dad went to the hardware store, picked up a roll of duct tape, and brought it back to the hospital. He ripped a piece of the truly all-purpose tape off of the thick, gray roll and slapped it on the top of my head. The stubble stung as it poked into my scalp and I lost my temper. I shot Dad a look that I thought would make him explain.

He didn't care. He didn't say a word. Too engrossed in his project, I guess. Pressing down the edges and corners of the tape, he then ripped the tape back off of my head.

"Ouch, Dad!" I growled.

Ignoring me, he looked at the sticky side of the tape and then turned it around. The duct tape was full of all the hairs that'd been trying to work their way out of my skin.

Dad smiled.

He repeated slapping tape on and ripping it off again and again. Some of the stubble came out easily, and some was more stubborn, but eventually all the slivers of hair ended up in a coil of gray in the trash can.

* * * * *

Slowly, the weekend passed, and the Mariners game had long ended with a homer by Griffey. Finally, late on Sunday afternoon my fever broke and temperature fell. The needle was pulled from my Port, and I put on my coat, shoes, and cap, ready to return to the Ronald McDonald House the second I was allowed. I waited for a nurse to come and take my temperature for the final time. Instead, here was Chad strutting in with the nurse's thermometer.

"Bend over!" he commanded.

Everyone laughed including Cherié, who'd followed him into the room. The nurse was behind her, and she playfully snatched the thermometer out of Chad's hands.

"Give me that thing," she said.

She slipped the thermometer under my tongue. It read 98.6 degrees.

"See you next time, Jason," she said.

Her voice trailed behind us as Chad and I passed her by and fled down the hall.

Our parents soon caught up. We were all going to visit Erik's room. Fearing other patients might make me sicker, or that I might share my sickness with them somehow, I hadn't visited with anybody else who had a weakened immune system. Even though Erik was just down the hall, I hadn't seen him while I was in for the fever. All weekend, though, Mom and Dad had reported that he looked healthy.

Erik was sitting up in his bed eating ice cream. The dark circles that usually hung beneath his eyes were swept aside, and his face was filled with new color. He greeted Chad and me with his usual smile, but it was brighter than normal. Rick and Sheri also looked revived. They were smiling brighter, too. I gathered why, when I overheard Sheri telling Mom and Cherié that it'd been a good week and an especially good day.

I didn't care that I was still in the hospital. My eagerness to leave went away the minute we arrived at Erik's door. I sat next to Chad near Erik's bed, happily listening to Chad's jokes and Erik's laugh. Looking at my two friends, a lengthy and frustrating weekend spent in the hospital turned into an encouraging afternoon.

I'd been released from my latest hospital visit, was feeling stronger and surer of my role in this new life with each passing day, and returning home to Montana wasn't as distant a dream. Chad was doing well enough to have a weekend away from the hospital visiting his friends at home, and for the first time since I'd been in Seattle, Erik was genuinely looking and feeling good. Cancer threatened each of us, for a time was inescapable, and seemed to be everywhere. But as we sat in the company of each other's encouragement, we surrounded the disease—and we defied it, every part of it.

Cancer could take away health, energy, fun, and even life. But it couldn't touch faith, love, courage—it couldn't touch our spirits. So, as we were forced to deal with cancer, it too was forced to deal with us. On this afternoon, the three of us joked and laughed. For a while we escaped the dark circles that cancer hung beneath our eyes, and the ache and nausea it hung on our bones and in our stomachs. It was the powerful disease that suddenly seemed to be a wimp.

To an outsider, it'd look like we were scraping on the bottom of life. But, on this Sunday, to ourselves, we couldn't have looked healthier: all three of us, but especially Erik. Erik, his doctors, and his family were in high hopes that this good week would continue into the next, then maybe a month, then a year. Right then, his progress gave both Chad and me a boost. Looking at Erik, we couldn't help but stand high above cancer. It couldn't ruin our perfect afternoon, and as long as we hung on to those moments, cancer couldn't touch us.

Chapter Sixteen

Questions for God

Tough times take so long to pass you by, a lifetime it sometimes seems. And the good times, the shiny moments, the ones where there's nowhere else you'd rather be, those ones are gone so fast. The harder I tried to hold on to the good ones, the quicker they slipped through my fingers. Like sand falling through my open hand, that sterling afternoon slipped by my friends and me. I couldn't hold on.

Chad and I left Erik's hospital room, but the laughter, rosy cheeks, and all around feeling of hope stuck with me. There was also a promise of more hope to come. We would see Erik soon. He was going to visit us for a change.

Because Erik's health had improved, he was able to spend the next afternoon away from his hospital room, and he chose to visit Chad and me at the Ronald McDonald House. Erik wouldn't be far from his hospital bed, but even one day at the McDonald House would break the never-ending chain of days he spent in the same room.

Chad had a radiation treatment that was going to overlap the first part of Erik's visit, but he promised I'd barely know he was gone.

"Be back in no time, Jay," he said.

I was sitting in the McDonald House's TV room when Erik and his mom arrived. Sheri wheeled him into the room and moved a dozen or so stuffed animals off a sofa, making a spot for Erik. He stood, pushed his wheelchair away, and sat down. Erik, Sheri, my parents, and I all sat on couches and chairs around the coffee table, ready to play a board game that Erik brought.

There were several large windows in the TV room that kept the cool out and let sunshine in all morning, so early afternoon was a nice time to be there. The day was bright and alive; rain and the spring sun fed fresh flowers and grass outside. And then the sun broke completely free of all clouds, lighting the room even more.

One beam of sunshine fell into the TV room through a skylight behind Erik, and cast its warm light on his back. Some of the sun absorbed into Erik's dark sweatshirt and some bounced off of his bald head. Whether reflected or absorbed, this bit of light was only interested in Erik. It didn't touch Sheri or me, even though we sat on either side of him. Creation shined a light on my friend, and Erik looked a bit brighter than the rest of us, indoors or out.

We rolled the dice, answered questions, and moved our game pieces around the board. Although we all gathered together around the game board and played the game, Erik was the center of attention. The spring light showed his laughter and the rosy color of his face. For a time it lit Erik's gladness and relief—later in the afternoon it lit his pain.

About halfway through the game Erik gasped and grabbed the armrest of the couch. He let go of the dice, spilling them onto the floor.

"Erik, are you okay?" Sheri asked.

"Yeah, it'll pass in a minute, Mom," he winced.

Sadly, the pain didn't pass. Sheri repositioned Erik on the couch. She leaned him to one side and then the other, she placed pillows on this side and then that, but nothing worked.

Erik's eyes were slammed shut waiting for the pain to go away, "Mom…we better get back to the hospital," he said.

"I think so, too," Sheri said, hastily scooping the dice from the floor and putting the game pieces and board back into the box.

Along with my parents, Sheri helped Erik into his wheelchair and the two of them left the house. Watching Erik climb weakly into his minivan made me sick to my stomach and afraid.

His family's van was the same as ours: an Aerostar, except his was green instead of gray. The green minivan circled the parking lot and pulled alongside the curb where I stood. He rolled down his window, ignored all pain, managed a smile, and let me know he'd be fine.

"Don't worry, Jason, we'll finish the game next time," Erik said.

"Next time," I repeated softly.

I didn't understand how he knew what to say, how he could let me know everything was under control when there were so many question marks in his life.

"What's wrong?" my mother asked me later.

"Nothing, Mom…I'm tired's all. Going to lay down in the room for a while," I said. "Can you make sure nobody wakes me?"

"All right, son," Mom said.

"Mom…"

"Yes?"

"Nobody," I asserted.

She nodded and I closed the door to our room.

I wasn't tired, but I didn't want to talk to anyone about anything, not even Chad. Alone in my room, I couldn't shake the painful look I had seen on Erik's face, not for a second. I'd caught a hint of the pain Erik's cancer caused and his disappointment when the hope of health was smashed. That's all Erik would let me catch though—just a hint.

That afternoon was the first time I'd seen cancer really get to Erik. Before, I'd seen the posters of baseball pitchers, NFL quarterbacks, and a picture from the cast of *Cheers* on the walls in his hospital room. I'd even thought about how strange it was that he had a couch near the foot of his bed. This was more than enough to know without a doubt that Erik was very sick, and he'd been in the hospital for a long time.

Questions for God

But, he'd never let me see cancer hurt him.

Erik spoke confidently about my treatments, the funny things he noticed about friends and family, the hospital, the sickness around us. He never spoke about pain or being sad. But then, I'd never gotten the whole story about his diagnosis or chemotherapy protocol. We only talked about my doctors' reports and scan results. From the first time we met, there wasn't a conversation you'd call "small talk." Yet there were jokes in every talk, no matter how serious the topic, and I always left Erik's room ready to fight another day.

Before I saw the pain on his face and we called off his outing to the house, Erik always made things seem like they were under control. His attitude made me look at his life with cancer the same way I looked at mine; I believed that this life of chemo and surgeries, needles and doctors, was temporary, an unpleasant solution to a unwelcome problem. Erik's pain and surprising exit from the Ronald McDonald House brought up more questions, awful questions: *maybe everything wasn't under control? Maybe this disease isn't temporary? Maybe Erik wouldn't survive?* It was the first time I'd had thoughts like these.

"Step-by-step" and "day-to-day" were truer than ever. It's like yelling in an empty room, a train station, a school gym, maybe a cave or even a big hole. Somebody that sounds just like you, but with a stutter, comes calling back, "Step-by-step…step…step…step. Day-by-day…day…day…day. Comparing this afternoon to the one before echoed what the doctors had told us about living in the short term. I now realized how quickly things change, how one day a patient stands high above cancer and the next is cruelly thrown down on the ground.

But the two afternoons also showed me that living "step-by-step" and "day-to-day" could completely trick you. I was so busy living every day and taking each step that I hadn't considered the longer term problem of maybe losing a friend. My understanding of cancer had grown immensely, but the thought of anyone's last breath, of anyone's last heartbeat, the reality of death, hadn't begun to sink in. I couldn't grasp the grave reality that allowed me to touch and talk to somebody one day, and then have them gone forever on the next.

I prayed, had a faith, believed in Jesus, and so did my friends. I knew they were sicker than me, but I believed Chad and Erik would beat cancer sooner or later. Looking past a day or two, beyond the difficulty or problem right in front of me, I glimpsed a bigger picture: people around me might really die. The possibility of Erik's death challenged the Bible stories I'd heard all of my life from the Sunday morning pulpit and from Dad's nightly readings.

My stomach sank for Erik, for the pain he was dealing with, and for the chance that his last breath and heartbeat were growing near. My stomach also sank because of a brand new selfish fear: I might die, too. Erik and I didn't just have a similar cancer; we both had Ewing's. I wondered if his pain that afternoon would be mine soon, if I could be close to an arm-chair-gripping pain, if next year I might have my last breath and heartbeat. And I wondered—*God…where are you? How do you fit in all of this?*

Reading and watching TV didn't help. Hiding my face in my pillow and praying didn't work either. I tossed and turned, but I couldn't escape the thoughts of Erik's death, my death, or find a loving God in all this sickness.

By evening, sitting alone in my room at the McDonald House overwhelmed me and pushed me close to a breaking point. I couldn't ignore the questions circling my mind. Instead of crying or screaming out loud, I walked outside to get some fresh air, to take a deep breath, and if only for a minute, clear my thoughts.

I sat in a park swing on the McDonald House's playground. The swing was made for a kid younger than me; the chains pressed against my hips, and the toes of my sneakers drug back and forth through the dirt under me. Sitting in the swing wasn't comfortable, but the night air and playground were a nice change.

Before I had switched off my TV, the weatherman had said that the clear night would make the cool, heavy air fall toward the ground, moving warmer, lighter air out of its way. Even though Harp had told me, "Never trust a weather prognosticator," I think the weatherman was right; a comfortable breeze blew against me. I leaned back in the swing, tilted my head, and scanned the sky. There wasn't one cloud. Stars stretched from the grove of trees behind me to the group of buildings in front; there were so many stars that counting them seemed impossible.

"Thought you were tired," my father said, stepping outside.

"Couldn't sleep," I replied.

He sat in an empty swing next to me, knees uncomfortably pressed to his chest. I leaned back and again looked up. "It's so big," I said.

Dad also looked at the sky. "It sure is," he replied.

He didn't ask or prod; Dad waited for me to tell him what was bothering me.

"I have some questions for Him, Dad," I said.

"Questions for who?"

"For God. Can I do that? Can I ask God questions?"

Dad smiled, still looking up at the night sky, "I think He's big enough, Jason."

After a few minutes of quiet, he spoke again, "You have to, Jason…God speaks to each of us differently, and asking questions lets God know you're searching for Him. Questions show him you're not lazy, and you care to hear what He might have to say. A guy has to question and find answers for himself, find out what he really believes. I just didn't think it was going to happen to you so soon."

"It doesn't fit anymore," I said.

"What doesn't?"

"Everything…heaven and Jesus…it doesn't fit anymore. How do I know all of those stories you read me from the Bible are really true?" As I asked, part of me was expecting a bolt of lightning to appear from the clear sky and strike me down.

"By questioning. By searching," Dad replied. "If you search for it, truth has a way of showing itself, even through the mire, son. There's a lot of tough stuff in our lives, and a lot more all over the world, but I believe there're pieces of a loving God in all of it…I think this trouble all around us will make you believe the same thing.

"When you do, the proof will be in your mind and your thoughts, in your heart, and it'll even sink into your bones. You'll say *AaaHa! I get it!* Then the difficulty isn't believing the Bible's real, or that God's real, or that He cares for you, but finding a way to describe all of it."

"But if God cares, then why's there so much tough stuff all over the rest of the world?" I asked. "Never mind the world…why's Erik so sick?"

"That's why we call it faith, Jason," he replied. "If it were called fact, there'd be no believing and life would be a simple problem: two plus two equals four. If life were only facts, there'd be no need for faith, and no room for miracles. But our lives, our God, and the world around us aren't easy math problems. They're real mysteries. Keep questioning and searching, give God some room, and you'll find answers."

"It'd be nice to know it all tonight, just like you. Then I'd go inside and fall asleep like I used'ta before," I said.

"I don't know it all, son…not tonight and not ever. There are no easy answers… not for you and not for me." His voice stern, "I have as many questions as you do. Mine are just different, that's all."

Taking a deep breath, Dad went on, "Jason, the world's pushing you to grow up faster than most, and Mom and I can walk alongside only so far." His voice calm again, he went on, "We can help you only so much in the hospital, and in your decisions of 'how' and 'what' to believe. Children think and act like children, but when we grow up, we're forced to put some childish ways behind us. There'll come a time when you see and understand like—"

"You going into another Bible story?" I interrupted.

"Yes."

"I don't want to hear any stories right now, Dad."

"No more stories tonight then."

* * * * *

A Look Back: Hope for an Answer

Like most boys, when difficult questions arose, I turned to my dad. However, his appreciation for life and reverence for God were too profound to offer trite answers. He would not strip anyone of their personal journey through life and the opportunity for divine wisdom just so they might have a temporal peace and sleep well at night. He provided a theological foundation from which others could draw answers. My father taught that answers would not come from him, but from God speaking through the Bible and through life.

This was especially true for my brother and me. Throughout my fight with cancer and in the years that followed, Dad taught us to stretch our minds' limits and try to understand—not how God fit into our character and circumstance, but how we fit into God's. He believed it was necessary to look to God with even the most difficult questions, because the focus moves beyond "self" and on to something bigger.

"Boys, when looking to God, you are no longer the measure, God is the measure," he often said to Jon and me.

I was measured all my life by parents, teachers, and coaches. They measured me through grades and goals. As I fought cancer, measurements changed—my health was obsessively measured by the analysis of blood counts, bone scans, and MRI machines. My health was measured against my peers' in Montana and my friends' at Children's. Because Erik and I had the same exact disease, the measurement of our cancer was separated by very little—by a word—relapse.

Compared to all of the other words I have had to learn in my life, relapse is probably the worst. It is the term used by doctors to tell a patient that a new tumor or the re-growth of an old tumor has occurred. "Relapse" measures the fickle nature of cancer, as a body can be clear of disease for months or years, and then one day a bone scan or MRI detects a tumor on a bone or in a lung. Erik had relapsed: there were tumors in his lungs and on his bones. I had no new or re-grown tumors, and I did not suffer the way Erik did.

On the day Erik's visit to the McDonald House ended and his suffering was no longer hidden from me, I feared his pain would not ease and he might soon die. Moreover, from that day on I feared one of my tests would show a relapsed tumor, setting me on a course further from my childhood in Montana, closer to the pain I had seen in Erik, and closer to my own death.

One recurring tumor changes hope for life into the fear of suffering and mortality.

"Relapse," and all the meaning the word carried with it, would turn restful sleep to nights of tossing and turning. Many of my dreams became nightmares so clear and frightening that I often woke gasping and sweating, believing I had relapsed.

Thoughts of death, and witnessing Erik's suffering, caused my measurements to change once again—from the medical to the spiritual. I struggled, stretched, and looked to God with questions.

When praying and asking these questions, my father believed it was important to approach God with the nature of a child, regardless of age. Asking, "Why?!" in anger or with entitlement was not how my brother and I were taught to approach God. We were to ask "Why?" from the innocence and unawareness of youth. I was to question with a belief that the space between the moon and me could be easily filled with the many things I did not know. The divine hand reaching out to our world is a gift simply referred to by my father as "grace."

"Boys, answers don't come from entitlement, but from grace," my father would say. "We don't deserve any of it, not Jesus, the cross, eternal life, or answers. They are all a gift—a gift we call God's grace."

Struck by the wound of grief, I have not always approached God with a handsome request. My prayers have not always been tidy and pretty. I have not always given the reverence deserved. I have gritted my teeth and called for answers from God. Often, I hear no reply.

Questions of death and love, pain and God, are not easily answered. I've never heard a thundering voice from heaven, never seen a burning bush or blinding light. I have never received an instantaneous answer when I angrily demanded it from God, nor when I prayed with reverence. The difficult questions that arose during my fight with cancer are questions I have been forced to live. In searching, experiencing, praying, and reading every day, in living the big questions, I do not dwell on conclusion but in the belief and hope that there is an answer.

As I sat on the McDonald House's swing set and contemplated cancer and death, my father did not ease my mind or answer my questions. But he left a foundation that allowed me to search and question for myself. He shoved the world away from me, clearing a space for spirituality to take root.

Chapter Seventeen

Lucky to Have Cancer?

Mom woke me. She said we were visiting the hospital to see how Erik was doing. I didn't want to go. I didn't want to see Erik.

I dreaded walking into his room. The previous afternoon had showed me what it's like to be a cancer patient as problems got even worse, and I didn't want to see a friend suffer or wonder if it'd soon be that bad for me.

My parents didn't know why it took me so long to get out of bed, why my shower was much longer than usual, or why I hung back in the elevator and hall outside of Erik's room. They naturally hurried to Erik's bedside, and I said nothing of my fears to them because I was ashamed.

Stopping outside of the door to Erik's room, I swallowed hard, put my head down and forced myself to walk inside. Erik lay back in his bed with eyes closed. I heard the beat of a respirator, pushing air into him…moment…by moment…by moment. He was getting oxygen through tubes in his nose. The tubes were necessary because relapsed tumors in his lungs resisted each breath.

The mechanical sound was eerie; the tubes unnatural. The tubes and sounds, threatening pain and death, pressed me against the wall just inside the door. I leaned against it and looked at the floor. Dad was next to Rick and Sheri, and Mom stood at the bottom of Erik's bed.

Mom rubbed Erik's feet, "How're you feeling?" I heard her ask.

"Better today," he sighed.

Erik slowly opened his eyes and scanned the room. When his gaze fell on me, he stopped. I felt his eyes, I looked up, and he waved me over to his bed. He pointed to the chair where I had been sitting just a couple of days ago when Chad, Erik, and I were enjoying that sterling afternoon. I walked past Mom and sat in that seat, silent, trying to think of something to say, something nice or cheery. Anything would do, but I said nothing.

"We're lucky, you know," Erik said, breaking the awkward silence. "Not everyone has the strength in them to handle cancer, Jason."

After a pause, he continued, "God only gives a person what they can handle. You and I fight this disease because we're strong. We won't allow cancer to break us, defeat us, no matter what."

Erik was soft-spoken, but sure, so sure that I couldn't look away. Listening intently to all he said, a particular word haunted me more than the rest. Erik told me he was "proud."

He didn't ask why God allowed this disease to eat him alive. Why he was the one who'd no longer play baseball or water ski. Why his strength was taken to the point of trading a toilet for a catheter, or his every breath dependent on oxygen tanks and tubes. Erik replaced "why" with "pride."

"God's plan is perfect," Erik said. "I can't understand it all now, but it's like a masterpiece, Jason. And I'm proud to be part of it."

Erik was like a brush of red on the sunset of a grand portrait, or a rose that completed a grand garden. But I think Erik was more than a rose. Anyone can find beauty in a rose or a sunset. To make the sickness all around us at Children's into something lovely would take something more than any person could come up with. It reminded me of some advice I heard Dad once tell a tough foster kid: it took the hand of our creator to make a thorn, nail, cross, broken body and bread, spilled blood, and wine into something beautiful.

In the hours since I'd seen all that ache on Erik's face while leaving the McDonald House, questions taunted me—I doubted God, grace, and heaven, beliefs I once held to be absolutely true. I wanted answers to my questions, answers that'd stop those doubts.

I wondered how Erik stayed calm, how he could comfort others while he was in so much pain, and be so sure or happy despite all the question marks. But Erik's faith was my answer. It satisfied my questions and doubts: from his certainty and encouragement welled his hope, and from there flowed the spring of his laughter and jokes.

Experiences came up that challenged my beliefs, but they were followed by others that, in the end, proved those beliefs. There was something terribly wrong deep inside of Erik, something that caused him pain and threatened his life. But something even deeper inside of him, something surpassing skin and bone, heartbeat and breath, caused me to leave his room on that morning stronger and surer of those Sunday morning stories than ever before—through life and questions, they were becoming more than just stories. Erik's faith was contagious.

Chapter Eighteen

Black Eyes, Bloody Lip, and a Bald Head

Chad's health kept on improving, and he was able to spend another weekend at home in Twisp. If everything went as planned, I'd also be home for a visit in a few days. I'd leave for Missoula before Chad returned to the McDonald House, so we wouldn't see each other for almost a month.

"I'll see you in a few weeks, Jay," Chad said, slamming the trunk of his car.

He walked to the driver's side, opened the door, and placed a pillow on the driver's seat; it boosted him high enough to see over the steering wheel.

"Your mom's letting you drive home?" I asked Chad.

"Of course!"

"Maybe I won't see you in a few weeks."

Chad was unimpressed, "Yeah, two weeks may be too soon."

He gave me a hug, so did his mother.

Cherié's hair was jet black; although short, her hair was straight and was just long enough up front to get in her eyes, time and again.

Combing her bangs to the side, she said, "Good luck in your treatment tomorrow."

"Thanks."

"So long, Jay," Chad said. "Call if you need anything."

"I will, Chad."

Chappie and Dr. Pendergrass were sending me home to Dr. Speckart and to the hospital in Missoula. I was going to have two chemotherapy treatments there, so I'd be home for at least part of the summer. I was so excited for my home and the summer, but my first three-day chemo treatment stood between me and my trip to Montana.

No matter what the season outside, everything seemed like winter when I was inside the hospital for treatment. There, things felt cold to the touch and the mood was sterile and white. Just as a painted smile on a clown's face hides his real expression, the hospital's plants, tropical fish tanks, toys, and brightly colored rooms tried to distract me from the discomforts of chemotherapy.

To try and make chemo warmer and more tolerable, I added my own distractions to treatment. I dressed in my most comfortable pajamas, replaced the hospital sheets with sheets from home, and topped the bed with that comforter my Uncle Greg had given. The hoax didn't last long, and my comforts vanished minutes after chemotherapy began.

Within fifteen minutes of chemo beginning to drip, I was reminded of the misery required to cure this disease. My body shook with nausea. I puked more in the first hours of this treatment than I had the entire five days of my previous one. In the first day of this treatment I puked more than I had in the first eleven years of my life, and by the end of the first night I'd puked more than Dad had in the first forty years of his life.

I lay on my side, curled up in a ball, clutching my stomach—still. Other than leaning over a bucket or urinal, my only movement came from my chest, as air moved in and out. My body was trying its best to give me every indication that it objected to being given this cure. My stomach and head were screaming to stop the poison I was allowing into my body. Ache pierced my bones until each felt broken, my bottom lip split because it was so dry and cracking, the blood vessels in my eyes burst because I puked so violently, and painful mouth sores developed on my tongue and cheeks. Before the three-day treatment began, my doctors had told me these drugs were stronger than those in my last treatment, but there was no way I could've prepared for this. It was agony from head to toe, and I wasn't the only person in my family who was tortured.

My parents were forced to sit back and watch my torment. Both Mom and Dad cried at the sight of my battle during this stay. They tried to hide their tears, leaving the room every so often, but I saw through their cover, even with my eyes closed. Their discomfort hurt me even more, but I didn't have the energy to cry. My entire being was directed toward hanging on for another moment.

I lost myself in the rhythm of my chest; a breath in, a breath out, each reminding me I was alive, and moving from one moment to the next. This became my protocol, my entire focus—until we found blood in my vomit.

Mom couldn't take it. She hit her breaking point and decided to put her foot down. She made the nurse page a doctor. Mom was convinced that this wasn't right. All her logic pointed to the conclusion that something must be wrong! My condition couldn't be normal, not even for a cancer patient. She believed the medical staff had given me a higher dose of the drugs than my body could handle. *Surely this must be a mistake?*

When Dr. Pendergrass arrived, he carefully looked over my reports, my medical chart, and the drugs I'd been given. Then he put his hand on my shoulder.

"Hang in there," he whispered.

The charts and doses were correct.

Dr. Pendergrass escorted my parents into the hall and spoke to them. I'm not sure what was said, but I guessed that he said something like "hang in there" to them, too.

It was difficult to hang in there when there was no real rest, nowhere to hide, and sickness never let up. I was too sick to focus on a TV or a video game, so my only escape was with books; the only break came through my imagination, the adventures I found between the covers of a novel.

Black Eyes, Bloody Lip, and a Bald Head

Mom and Dad read tirelessly, transporting me to the clouds, the battlefield, the ocean, and Narnia. Thoughts, ideas, pages, and chapters crafted years before by strangers seemed to be written for the sole purpose of getting me through my sickness and the boredom of chemotherapy.

My parents took turns reading, even whispering at night, helping me to "hang in there." I did—three nights passed and the treatment ended. Chemo came to an end once again; I'd finished my second treatment.

A nurse wheeled me out of the hospital room. I waved at my roommates. Nausea came rapidly, fiercely at the beginning of this treatment, and I hadn't spoken or even really noticed them since it began. Each of them probably wished they could say the same. I had made quite a racket, and from the ghastly look on each one of their faces, I gathered they were surprised I was leaving, at least so soon, in one piece, and sitting upright.

Little did they know I was propped up: I held my head in one hand and grabbed the armrest of the wheelchair with the other. Hunched over in the chair, my stomach muscles ached with exhaustion from vomiting, I had a bloody lip and two big black eyes from broken blood vessels. Cotton balls, once white but slowly bleeding red from the sores, filled my mouth. They kept my cheeks and tongue from touching each other or my teeth, making the sores in my mouth bearable. I was beat up and didn't show my relief from reaching the end of this three-day treatment.

I could see that Erik was a bit taken back when the nurse wheeled me into his room. He shook his head, "It never stops shocking you, Jason," he said, more nasally than usual because of the oxygen tubes in his nose.

"No...it doesn't," I slurred through the cotton balls.

"You going back to Montana for a while?" Erik asked.

"I leave in—," I took the cotton balls out of my mouth before finishing, "in the morning."

"Better get going," Erik laughed, "before you fall outta that wheelchair."

I looked closely at Erik for a sign of him maybe getting better, or maybe worse.

"I'll be here," he said without waver. "See you when you get back, Jason."

"See you in a few weeks," I nodded, delicately re-stuffing the sticky cotton between my cheeks.

The next morning Mom, Dad, and I left the Ronald McDonald House for our trip home. My parents had everything packed up by the time I woke up. Dad had made a small bed for me in the back of our van and promised there'd be only a short interruption in my rest.

I rose and dressed, walked to the van, and climbed inside. I laid down in the back seat, on my big green-and-blue comforter. Mom had just washed and dried it to get rid of the hospital smell. The morning was cool, but my comforter was still warm. The seat was more comfortable than the bed in the McDonald House, and it was easy to rest again.

Before closing my eyes, I noticed a bag on the floor. It was a red, white, and blue duffle bag. I hadn't opened the bag even once since we arrived in Seattle, which was unusual because it was full of my favorite toys. There were about a hundred plastic army men in that bag, and I'd completely forgotten about them. As Dad shifted the car into drive, I unzipped the bag and dug until I found my favorite plastic hero. I sat, figure in hand, looking at the toys.

I'd looked forward to going home since we'd left for Seattle, and my longing for Missoula had grown whenever a memory of home arose, or when I compared life before cancer to all the days since my diagnosis. Now, finally on my way, the unthinkable happened—I was surer of the city I was leaving than the home I was going back to. I'd grown to trust my doctors in Seattle, the strange protocol and routine at Children's. More than anything, I'd grown to trust my friends who fought beside me. There's an unspoken closeness when aches and pains, loves and hates, days and sleepless nights are so similar. In one glance there was understanding between us. Chad and Erik were a part of my life for a short time, but we had similar scars and the same fears—through cancer, a strong friendship was cemented between the three of us.

I'd known my family and many of my friends in Montana since birth, but we'd never faced something like cancer, so we'd never been forced to beat it together. I'd be accepted and loved in Missoula, but without Chad and Erik something was missing. At home there'd be no one on my side of the needles, on my side of the sickness.

Dropping the plastic army man back into the bag, I zipped it up for good. The toys weren't fun to play with anymore. Because of cancer, I now lived in a grown-up situation with grown-up punishments. In the time I'd been away from Montana, I had become different. My routine, the way I looked at things, and the way I looked, period, had changed. It just took one look at my reflection in the van window to see that. Pale skin and black eyes, bald head and a thinned body—I barely recognized the boy staring back at me. This image made me wonder. Like me, had home changed, too?

* * * * *

"Who wants to kiss the cook?" Harp belted out.

The scene of our family gathering for dinner at my Grandma Dorie and Grandpa Harp's house in Missoula was exactly the same—dinner and dessert, spilled drinks and old jokes, and afterwards, just like normal, Harp ran head-on into the coffee table while taking out the garbage. *Whack!* The table shook as it collided with his shin. He dropped the trash, hopped around for a minute on one foot, and then yelped towards the kitchen.

"I don't know why you put this damn thing here, Dorie!" he exclaimed, as if the table had moved in the last fifty years.

As usual, my grandmother grumbled under her breath, and I laughed aloud.

On our way home from my grandparents, I knew each block, house, fence and tree. I knew the lamp light in our front yard, our house's simple rectangle frame, and the jingle of my father's keys as he opened the front door.

The familiarity of this place appealed to a piece of me that I didn't understand, except to say it was home. The air was sweeter, the bed sheets felt softer, and a stress I didn't realized I'd been carrying drained from my neck and shoulders. Never before had I fallen asleep so fast, or rested so deeply.

Waking up in my hometown, in my own house, at the beginning of summer was better than I'd dreamt. Not long after I got home, I awoke to my twelfth birthday. Our return from Seattle landed almost exactly on my birthday.

My family and grade-school friends planned to meet at my grandparents' house for cheeseburgers and cake to celebrate. Jon and I pulled our bicycles from the garage. I dusted mine off and we rode to Grandma Dorie and Grandpa Harp's house well

Black Eyes, Bloody Lip, and a Bald Head

before the party began. It was only a four-block ride, but I was so weak, I was out of breath and dizzy in no time. I slowed down and almost stopped before I fell off my bike, but still I scraped the palm of my hand.

"You hurt?" my brother asked.

I clapped my hands together, knocking the gravel from my palm.

"Just a scratch, Jon."

When we got to my grandparent's house, Grandma Dorie cleaned up the scrape, wiped it down with antiseptic, and wrapped it in a clean bandage. It wasn't enough. Within minutes I had red streaks halfway up my arm. An infection was taking over my body. My blood counts were too low, and my immune system couldn't fight anything off.

Mom called Dr. Speckart. I needed to go to the emergency room, and that's where I ended up spending my birthday: in the hospital. While the friends I'd grown up with were eating birthday cake, my port-a-cath was accessed and I was hooked up to an IV bag full of antibiotics.

This hospital stay wasn't long. I was able to leave the emergency room hours later, but by then my birthday party was over.

That night I called the McDonald House to hear a familiar voice.

"How was your trip home, Chad?" I asked.

"Happy birthday Jay!" Chad said. "You never guessed by twelve you'd be balder than your dad, huh?"

"Yeah, happy birthday," I commented and proceeded to tell him about my day. Even though he must have understood, he showed no sympathy.

"Well, if you're good, maybe you'll get another one next year," Chad said, pissing me off and making me laugh at the same time. Then, he got more serious, and I settled in, knowing some advice was on the way, "Jay, I've got this, like, bubble around me."

"A bubble?" I asked.

"When bad things like infections or relapsed tumors want to get me, they bounce off," he said, "and what keeps the bubble strong are prayers from all of the churches and my positive thoughts—the bad things can get me, but they can never really get *to* me, you know?"

"I shouldn't let this stuff get to me?" I asked

"Bingo."

"Alright, Chad, I got it," I said. "How'd your tests go?"

Chad's latest scans all came back clear, which was really great after years of relapsing tumors. But then Chad told me some bad news. Erik's health was worse. His tumors were multiplying, and it was becoming harder for him to breathe.

Chad told me Erik was on a new kind of oxygen machine, one with a mask that covered all of his nose and mouth.

"Erik's too stubborn to talk through that mask," Chad said. "He took it off and tried to talk to me normally. Guess he didn't want to sound like Darth Vader or something. My mom finally made me leave so Erik'd put the mask back on, 'cause it looked like he was gonna pass out or something."

Even in the worst times, Erik dealt with cancer on his own terms.

Chad described Erik's bad condition in a way that lightened the news. He made me smile while we talked. But after I hung up the phone, sadness stayed with me until bedtime.

As Dad read and Mom tucked me in, each noticed something was wrong.
"Can I help?" my father asked.
"Don't think so, Dad."
"Are you feeling alright, Jase?" Mom asked a while later.
"Yeah…just tired."
"Well, I'm right across the hall if you need me."
I reached over to turn off the lamp.
"I know. 'Night, Mom."

Even after what I'd been through at the Children's Hospital in Seattle, I took much of my life for granted. I shared a disease with people who didn't count on another birthday. For Chad and Erik, the arrival of another birthday was a gift to be thankful for, all on its own, no matter where they were spending it. Burying my head in my pillow, I prayed for Chad and Erik. I'd prayed for them most nights since we met, but this was the first time I asked God for the big one—a miracle.

Please give Chad and Erik a miracle, Jesus. Please take their cancer away from them…Amen.

I gave that prayer everything I had, putting as much thought and heart into it as I possibly could. Shutting my eyes and holding my breath, I heaved my prayer to heaven with all the strength inside me. When I could hold my breath no longer, I stopped praying, rolled over and stared at the ceiling. Exhaling loudly, I decided right then, I'd never again pray for anything but miracles.

Chapter Nineteen

Home for a Visit

Unlike life at Children's Hospital, Missoula's change continued at a natural speed. Spring moved to summer, and with it came cut-offs, T-shirts, and more relaxed routines. School was out and September was far away. The days fit nicely into the cycle that I had known so well year after year. The trouble was, I didn't quite fit at the hospital in Missoula, or anywhere else in town.

There were goods and bads about being different. Anything within reason that I asked for, I got, without question. I could eat ice cream and sugary cereal at any time of day, because my parents were just happy I was well enough to eat. Also, when my blood counts were high enough to be around other people, my parents expected me to get out of the house and spend time with friends.

"Mom, can Matthew and I go to—"

"Yes!" my mother happily answered before I could even finish asking.

Unfortunately, there were also comments from stupid people and blank stares from strangers. Chad and I had been stared at in Seattle, but not as often, and Chad liked to stop whatever he was doing to stare back. He liked to watch the faces of those strangers when they realized they were gawking at a sick kid. That shifted any feelings of being a misfit away from us and put them back on the stranger.

I wasn't as bold as Chad, but pretty soon I settled into using my appearance to my advantage. Often I could be caught staring back at strangers, alerting them of their stupidity. Other times I used my bald head, dark circles beneath my eyes, and the need to wear a surgical mask, which kept germs from entering my body, to get fast service or go to the front of long lines.

"Are you contagious?" a stranger might ask.

"Oh, yeah, you may not want to stand too close," I'd reply, while coughing in their direction.

Amazingly, my way would be cleared.

The reactions of other kids were the most obvious. There was no need for guessing or looking for hints in what they did. Children pointed or laughed, and would just ask, "Where's your hair?"

I rarely answered honestly, though. "Had a scary nightmare last night, and woke up like this," I told some kids. "Stuck a fork in a light socket," I told others.

I also borrowed a good one from Chad: "My body hair slowed me down, so I had it removed."

The pleasant waves and pats on the back that I got from Missoula's caring residents far outweighed anything else I experienced from rude people. It was so unusual to see a cancer kid around my town that everyone in Dr. Speckart's office and the staff at Missoula's Saint Patrick's Hospital knew my name, and they treated me like a king when I was in for treatment. I quickly trusted Dr. Speckart and the hospital staff as much as anyone at Children's Hospital.

The two treatments I had at home were no easier or harder than those in Seattle. I was in a different place, but the drugs and my body's reaction to them was the same. Throughout my fight with cancer, my five-day treatments made me nauseous, my body weak, and my bones ache. The time during these treatments seemed long and drawn out. I'd just watch the clock and wait for the end of the five days; it was the waiting during my five-day treatments that was harder than the sickness, weakness, and pain.

Three-day treatments were a whole different story. Because they were shorter, I didn't have the agony of waiting and watching the clock. But the misery—I don't know what else to call it—during these treatments was far worse than the five-day treatments. Violent puking often caused me to leave the hospital with eyes blackened from broken blood vessels. I would bring a heating pad because my bones ached so badly. By the end of the three days, I'd have several mouth sores.

What I went through in the hospital for both the five-day and three-day treatments allowed me to appreciate summer days spent at home and outside the hospital that much more. Montana's sun browned my skin and kissed my head with freckles, making me look less pale and sick. Sometimes during that summer I almost felt like life was the same as it'd been before.

I spent many summer days with my brother and friend Matthew, riding our bicycles and swimming in the river. One afternoon, Matthew, Jon, and I rode our bikes to the baseball fields in our neighborhood to play a game of home-run derby. On the short ride to the field, I carried a small wooden baseball bat we needed for the game. Jon rested a five-gallon bucket full of baseballs on the handlebars of his bike, and Matthew carried all three of our mitts.

There were about a dozen baseball fields right behind my elementary school. Each field was surrounded by a chain-link fence. They were well kept, with soft grass and a cushion of dirt along the baseline. As long as we could find a field where the sprinklers weren't on or a little league game wasn't being played, we were welcome to use them. The field we picked was empty, and although the grass was damp from being watered, no sprinklers were running.

"What're the rules?" Jon asked.

"One outfielder, one pitcher, one batter," I said. "The batter gets nine swings and then we switch."

"Person with the most homeruns wins," Matthew added. "Who's going first?"

"One of you guys can," Jon said, walking out to right field.

"You can go first, Jason," Matthew said.

Home for a Visit

Matthew stood on the pitcher's mound with the bucket of baseballs and lobbed one to me. I swung and missed.

Matthew and I didn't talk over a beer or a cup of coffee like grown-ups, but when we were playing, there was time for discussion. I knew I looked different since I'd been to Seattle, and my life and routine weren't the same as Matthew's anymore, but the great thing was, he didn't treat me all that differently. We still talked about baseball cards, videogames, and occasionally—girls.

"That girl on the other side of the park liked me," Matthew said, grabbing another ball from the bucket.

"The one driving the black car?" I asked, tapping the plate with the wooden bat and then getting ready to swing once again.

"That's the one," Matthew answered.

Matthew lobbed a second ball, making it easy for me to hit. I swung and again missed.

"Hey, you guys! Jon should only get five swings!" I yelled.

"Why don't I get nine?" Jon yelled back from right field. "Because you have cancer?"

"No, dummy!" I hollered. "Because you're way bigger than us!"

"Oh…," Jon thought for a moment. "Whatever, I'll only take five swings," he agreed.

"The girl in the black car, huh? She looked like way older…graduating high school or somethin'?" I was back to the original subject.

"Well, I saw her looking over at us. Probably checking me out…now that I think about it," Matthew said. "We know she wasn't looking at Jon."

"Shut up, Matt!" my brother yelled. "Just 'cause I'm in outfield doesn't mean I can't hear!"

"Maybe she was looking at me," I said, pulling down the bill of my baseball cap, making sure it fit snugly and hid my bald head.

Matthew pounded the leather baseball glove with his fist a few times, his thoughts turning toward my cancer.

"You think it'll grow back?" he asked.

"What? My hair?" I asked, stepping away from home plate and taking a practice swing.

"Yeah, what else?" Matthew said.

"It'll grow back once chemo's finished."

"You sure? Grandpa Harp's never grew back!" my brother hollered from outfield.

"His fell out 'cause he was old, not 'cause of chemo," I answered sharply.

"Anyways, how much longer will you be home before you've to go back to Seattle?" Matthew continued.

"Week or so," I answered.

"When'll you come home next? Will you be back for school?"

"Dunno. It all depends if my tests and scans come back clear, and how it goes after my allograft."

"Allo—who?" Matthew asked, stumbling over the term.

"A shoulder surgery I'm having when I go back to Seattle."

I stepped back into the batter's box. "Pitch me the ball."

Matthew grabbed a baseball from the bucket and threw it straighter and faster than before. I swung and hit the ball hard.

The bat made a satisfying *crack!* and Matthew turned his head, looked up and pointed, following it over the outfield and out of the park.

My brother didn't move. He leaned against the chain link, legs crossed and both of his elbows resting on the top of the outfield fence. The ball landed in the grass just behind him.

"One-nothing!" Jon announced.

* * * * *

A Look Back: The World Forever Different

Puberty. A first love. Sex. Marriage. Divorce. Tragedy. It only takes a moment to experience events so monumental that they cause a paradigm shift—a change inside ourselves and how we relate to the world around us. These experiences seem to make the very ground we walk on quake, and life is fractured into a clear before and after.

Diane, my nurse from Children's, was correct, "It'll all still be there when you get home." And it was: my family and my neighborhood, good friends, the Clark Fork River splitting our town in two, and all the other charms that set the stage for my sweetest memories. Home had not changed, but my place in it had.

When I was diagnosed with cancer as a fifth-grader, I was innocent and naïve, yes, but I was not guiltless. I had cussed and lied, been in fistfights on the playground, and I had even been a thief. (Matthew and I once stole a Playboy *magazine from a Missoula bookstore because we wanted to know what all the fuss was about.) I was far from a perfect child and already in need of God's grace.*

However, cancer was the beginning of something different, a genesis: my tempting red apple plucked from the Tree of Knowledge, and my first real taste of good and evil. Innocence had been shattered, and though faith and a deep appreciation for life would allow me to pick up some of the pieces and paste them back together, childhood did not look quite like it had when it was new. The changes inside me while fighting cancer were so catastrophic, that I began viewing and interacting with my surroundings differently. Now, my life is referred to in terms of what occurred before and after my diagnosis with cancer.

During the summer of 1991 I had my allograft surgery. The bone transplant and the time I spent at Children's Hospital that summer held events that drove a significant shift in me, and in my perception of life. The shift had less to do with the actual surgery or its results, and more to do with my friendship with Chad and Erik.

Even so, at the time of the allograft I put a great deal of emphasis on the surgery because I truly believed that the doctors would be seeing my bone, not through a test or scan but with their own eyes. I believed they would be able to tell me if I had relapsed—if any new or regrown tumors had attached to my diseased collarbone. This perception was not entirely correct. Technology actually has a better chance of detecting cancer than the naked eye. Regardless, this period of my fight was important. And not just to me. It was also considered very important by the Children's Hospital staff taking care of me, and by my parents.

Years later I learned about a conversation between my doctors and a few nurses in the cafeteria at Children's. The topic of conversation was, among other things, my health. Doctors and

Home for a Visit

nurses all agreed that they would probably find a relapsed tumor during the allograft or testing I was to receive in Seattle that summer. Later, my mother would also tell me that she and my father were equally concerned.

On the day of the allograft, she was even more afraid than in the past months. Living life day-to-day was not enough to divert my mother's attention from the fear of my death. While I was still under anesthetic, she and my father had a moment alone in our minivan, and my mother told him how frightened she was.

"Do you have any peace?" she asked Dad. "Do you have the feeling everything's going to be fine, our prayers are going to be answered, and Jason will live?"

My father drove in silence. His answer was not the one my mother desperately wanted to hear.

"No," he replied, "I have no peace. I'm not sure what's going to happen. I don't know if Jason will live."

Choking back tears, Mom said, "Me either."

Chapter Twenty

You're Gonna Make It

The "summer sometime" arrived. It was July, and the allograft, that surgery that seemed so far off when I started fighting cancer, was now only days away. I'd finished more than three months of chemotherapy, and treatment looked like it was working because there were no new or regrown tumors in my body. It sounded like the simplest thing: no more cancer and a successful allograft, and I'd be finished with chemotherapy and disease in a little over a year. But it wouldn't be as easy as it sounded. My doctors said over and over again how important the allograft and the rest of my treatment were for surviving.

Jon, my parents, and I were going back to Seattle again. Leaving Missoula before my allograft was a lot easier than leaving the first time, just after diagnosis. For me, going back to Seattle meant I'd see Chad and Erik, and I'd be around those few who understood my sickness.

We arrived in Seattle at the Ronald McDonald House, and right away I went looking for Chad. I was excited to see him and I walked fast, almost jogging down the hall to the kitchen and then to the teen room. There he was, watching a recording of a late-night talk show. He was lying back on the couch with his feet up, pointing the remote control at the TV.

"Dumb VCR—it was supposed to record Letterman not Leno," he was saying.

I tried to not show how excited I was to see him, so I slowed my step.

"Hey Chad," I said calmly.

Unlike me, Chad wasn't at all embarrassed about showing his feelings. He shot off the couch and threw an arm around me. "Jay! I'm glad you're back! It hasn't been the same around here without you, man!" he said excitedly.

Just like my friends back home, Chad and I didn't talk over beer or coffee, but we talked a lot when were at the McDonald House or hanging out at our favorite places in Seattle. Unlike my friends at home, we talked about harder stuff, even by adult standards. We talked about surgeries and chemotherapy more often than cute girls and baseball cards.

A few hours after we got back to Seattle, and after my family unpacked a car full of stuff into our room at the Ronald McDonald House, Chad and I met back in the teen room. We began playing pinball, trying our best to beat the machine's highest score. While the pinball machine dinged and rattled, there was a feeling of belonging, and though I was a long way from Missoula, there was also a feeling of being close to home. But there was another feeling sinking in—a closeness to death. Chad was telling me that I was about to lose my first friend to cancer.

"Jay, Erik's at the end, you know?" he said. "Without a miracle, he's going to die. No more being shy, Jay. When we go visit, tell him whatever you're thinking. You might not get another chance. Sometimes those moments are just…kinda precious…you can't never get them back again."

Chad spoke purely, sincerely; the pain he felt from letting go of Erik as he'd let go of friends in the past was obvious. He didn't make this easy for me. Chad didn't joke or lighten any of it with any kind of hopeful advice. He gave the facts because he wanted me to know how important the time we'd spend with Erik would be, and what to expect when he and I visited Erik's room.

"His lungs are too full of cancer, Jay. Pretty soon he just won't be able to breathe anymore," Chad explained.

To die from this disease wasn't pleasant. Death wouldn't find our friend comfortably sedated. It'd be a bitter fight until the end. I learned that Erik would struggle until there was no life left in his lungs. Erik was going to "suffocate." Chad made me understand that Erik wouldn't have much comfort or peace when he went.

I got it. And I also understood that there wasn't much comfort or peace for the people who loved Erik, either. According to the experts, cancer was going to suffocate Erik, leaving a mom and dad without a son, a grandma and grandpa without a grandson, two older brothers without a younger brother, and one younger brother without an older brother. Chad and I were losing our friend, and the rest of the world was going to lose a light, which would dim the whole thing ever so slightly.

* * * * *

Standing outside of Erik's room on the second floor of Children's Hospital, Chad grabbed my arm. "How you doing, Jay?" he asked.

"Good," I replied. "Good."

My stomach twisted with nervousness and my heartbeat thumped loudly in my ears as we walked through the door.

The room was filled with Erik's family and friends. I don't think another person could've fit around his bed. The red couch was filled with people squeezed in from armrest to armrest, and the circle continued around both sides of Erik, carrying on to the head of his bed. It was a big ring of loved ones whose gaze was never far from the boy each of them had come to see.

I stopped outside the circle. The people naturally parted for Chad, and he didn't hesitate in sitting down next to Erik.

Chad leaned in close and began to tell a joke. "So there were two doctors, a nun, and a donkey named Hank," he said softly.

Everyone smiled. I bashfully followed Chad's lead, walking through Erik's family and friends.

I sat next to Chad but didn't speak. Instead I listened. Erik didn't speak either, because the tumors in his lungs made it nearly impossible for him to find the wind for even one word. An oxygen mask covered his nose and mouth, and even with that, every breath was a struggle. His chest wheezed in and out.

Chad filled any quiet spaces, scattering jokes in between stories, and he wasn't at a loss for words, not even for a moment. Though Chad may have been talking to Erik, he entertained everyone in the room. But just before he left, Chad leaned in to hug Erik, and quietly said something meant for the two of them.

Then Chad spoke a little louder. "See you soon," he said.

He stood, and the circle again parted as Chad walked confidently, without looking back, out of Erik's hospital room.

I moved to the seat where Chad had sat. I thought of the conversation Chad and I had, and I knew how precious the minutes with Erik truly were. Still, I didn't know what to say. A million thoughts and questions piled up in my mind. In but a second there was a traffic jam of "Thank you," "Why you?," "I don't know," and "Please don't go." Frustrated, I didn't know where to start, so I sat silent. Every time I opened my mouth to say something, my lips formed nothing.

Erik's graceful way helped the situation, and again he knew exactly what to do to make something difficult much easier. Reaching over, he took my hand in one of his, and with the other signaled for his mother to take the oxygen mask off of his face. With bloodshot eyes, Sheri approached the bed and moved the mask. My bottom lip began to quiver as he clinched my hand, pulled me close to him, and with all the breath he could muster, tried to speak.

"You're gonna make it," he whispered.

His words had no more volume than an exhale, but because of what he said, they might as well have been an earthquake. There'd be no forgetting them, not those words—not ever.

Through a screen of tears, I nodded in agreement. He gave my hand a final squeeze and then let it go. That was the last time that I'd ever see Erik.

Chapter Twenty-One

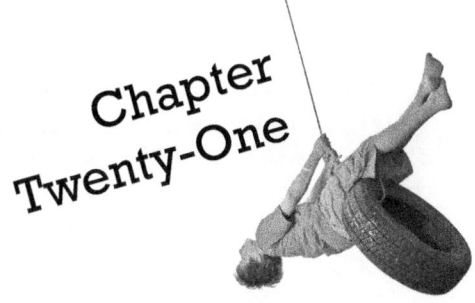

Death Came to Stay

"Are you ready?" a nurse asked.

Knowing it was time for my allograft sent shivers down my spine.

"Yes, ma'am," I replied shakily.

I was at odds sitting in the waiting room and prep area on the day of the surgery. On the one hand, the wait was agonizing, and on the other, I welcomed the delay. Part of me wanted to be in the operating room as soon as possible. Another part wanted to glue myself to the chair where I sat, pushing away the discomforts and uncertainty ahead. This day was important, big time important.

My collarbone was going to be cut out of my body, a donor bone put in its place, and a plate with eight screws attached to keep the new bone from moving. The outcome of the allograft would determine how much I'd be able to move my arm and how much pain I'd have in my shoulder for the rest of my life. More importantly, because doctors were going to see where my cancer had grown with their own two eyes, I believed the surgery would tell me how long that life would be. In my mind, survival depended on what they'd tell me when I woke up from anesthetic.

Seeing Erik at the end of his year-long battle with cancer, to me, confirmed that "relapse" was another word for "death." The allograft was a "fill in the blank." This hole in the sentence would be filled with an answer: *hope*—from a successful surgery and a body free from disease, or *relapse*—finding more cancer.

Just as they'd done for my "small surgery" in Missoula, my parents again walked alongside the bed as we moved toward an operating room. Mom and Dad each held one of my hands for as long as they could. Each of them would've gladly taken my place, but when we reached the two steel doors, yet again, my parents could walk no further. The doors separated the rest of the hospital from the operating room, and the person fighting this disease from everyone else walking alongside.

The doors opened to a cold room where everything looked like it was made out of stainless steel. Except for a few people from the medical team standing here and there, and an operating table that stood alone in its center, the room was nearly empty. Voices in the room bounced off the bare walls. I don't think anybody could really understand what it was like for me right then, not without being in my skin, at least. But the voices and the room's empty appearance was an image that helped express what it felt like inside me.

I lay on the operating table, cold. I think goose bumps must be a requirement for every medical procedure. A bright light directly overhead blurred my sight, making everything else out of focus.

"Good morning, tough guy," a familiar voice said.

The light shining in my eyes was redirected with the effortless tip of five long fingers. Chappie stood over me.

"Shall we get this over with?" he asked.

"I don't know."

A doctor standing next to Chappie pushed anesthetic into my IV. I lifted my head, making a statement not only to Chappie but to everyone in the room.

"You guys take good care of me," I said.

I tried to sound sure and confident, as I imagined Chad or Erik would've been. But as soon as I said it, I knew I sounded like a scared little boy.

* * * * *

A Look Back: The Allograft

An allograft is the surgical process of transplanting an organ or tissue from one individual of the same species to another, such as from human to human. Hundreds of thousands of allografts are performed every year in the United States. Presently, the surgery is used extensively in orthopedics, dental surgery, plastic surgery, and neurosurgery. Bone transplants have been common for many years, however, the popularity and successful use of allografts is relatively recent.

Before 1970, most people with sarcomas like mine were treated with amputation. The founding of The American Association of Tissue Banks in 1976 facilitated cell and tissue quality and quantity, helping meet transplant needs in the United States. The National Transplant Act passed in 1984, legalizing a first-come-first-serve basis for organ recipients and outlawing the purchase or sale of organs. This regulation further enabled the practice of transplanting organs, including bones, from one human being to another. Efforts by bone banks to use blood tests and other screening processes ensured that clean bones were available for transplants, which made allografts safer.

Resources needed to meet the high demand for surgery became available, making it possible for researchers and surgeons to begin perfecting the art of the bone allograft.

Many kinds of allografts preceded my surgery, but I was one of the first patients in history to receive a clavicular allograft.

The majority of my clavicle was removed; all that remained of my bone were the growth plates on each end. A donor bone was taken from a cadaver and placed inside my body. A long, thin, stainless steel plate and eight screws were fastened, attaching what was left of my bone to the donor bone. Chappie hoped my growth plates would grow over the donor bone, completely cover it, and in a sense, make it my own. If my body did, in fact, accept and cover the donor bone, the plates and screws could one day be removed.

On July 17, 1991, Chappie performed the allograft on my shoulder during a procedure that lasted about six hours. The allograft was considered a success: no new cancer was detected, I had an acceptable range of motion following the surgery, and though some pain would always be present, it was not unbearable. I was fortunate.

* * * * *

I woke up hurting. "Uuuuhhhh," I groaned.

My legs, neck, back, shoulder, and head burned with every variety of pain. Nausea was my body's response. I rolled to one side and puked on the floor. My vomit alerted a young nurse who placed a bucket and a rag by my head.

"Where am I?" I asked. "Where're my parents?"

"You're in Intensive Care. And your parents aren't allowed to come in yet. Jason, do you have any pain?" she asked.

"Yes," I choked.

"Where does it hurt?"

"Everywhere."

I tossed and turned but my movement made pain and nausea worse, so I lay still until the nurse returned.

"This will make you feel better," she said, attaching a morphine pump to the tube running from my Port.

The nurse started walking away, but I stopped her.

"Ma'am…what'd the doctors find?" I asked.

I knew she wasn't allowed to answer. It'd be my parents or doctors who'd tell me the surgery's results—if it'd gone well or if I'd relapsed. I wanted to read her body language, her tone, to see if she squirmed or if she smiled.

"Try and get some rest for now," she said, her eyes veering away from mine.

I'd become good at reading people's reactions, and hers made me sure something was wrong.

Hours later I woke up moaning again, "Uuhhhgg…" I paused for a moment, then realized, "This isn't so bad."

I didn't have the intense pain of before. The morphine pump must've helped. I wasn't in Intensive Care anymore, either. Instead, I was happy to find myself in a normal hospital room for three patients. I looked at my shoulder, at my feet, and then around the room.

Tubes ran from almost every part of my body; I looked more like one of the Hospital's fish tanks than one of its patients. There were two IVs in my right arm, one in my left, one in my foot, my Port was accessed, and a prayer crossed my mind as I hoped the catheter coming from underneath the sheets was delicately placed.

Mom sat in a chair by my bed. She was pale, there were bags under her eyes, and her cheeks were wet from crying.

"What's going on, Mom?" I asked, once more looking at all the tubes.

"Surgery took longer than the doctors expected," she said. "It took six hours and they needed extra IVs to keep you medicated, Jase."

"What'd they find?" I asked.

"Chappie said the surgery couldn't have gone any better. No signs of any new cancer."

I sighed and sank further into the hospital bed.

Cancer is tricky—, I don't even think my doctors could predict what it was really going to do. I'd seen how fast good things could turn bad, how brand new problems could throw me on the ground in a second. I felt like before the surgery, we faced an incomplete sentence. After, we had a fine answer: the blank in the sentence was filled with the word "hope."

I believed Mom. It was good news all around, really good. Still, there was a chill in her voice and a blood red tint in her eyes that scared me. Her words should've made me sit up and cheer. But like the nurse in Intensive Care, her appearance and a quiver when she spoke made me sure something was wrong. She knew something.

The air was filled with a scare that set my skin hot with anger.

"Mom!" I demanded.

Her voice trembled as she grabbed my hand.

"Erik's dead."

Mom cried. I just stared at her, not sure if I wanted to hear anymore.

She waited for Dad, and then they carefully described the final hours of Erik's life. The story amazed me—I reached out to catch a runaway breath, a lump rose in my throat, and butterflies fluttered in my pounding chest.

It seems strange because Erik was so young, but I'd met Erik in the autumn of his life. I'd seen his days growing shorter and colder. Death was like a shadow that'd grown longer. And as autumn brings the passing leaves and beauty of fall colors, Erik's passing brought with it a striking blend of love, grace, and miracles.

Cancer took his breath and his battle ended, but Erik wasn't beaten. Like the faithful before him, Erik was tested, but it only made him stronger. A murdering disease took his strength, his home, and life, but he wouldn't let cancer break his spirit. In this dark and muddy world of cancer, God's face shone brightly.

Chad turned out to be wrong, because Erik didn't suffocate. It was just the opposite. For the first time in months, Erik's voice wasn't strained, and color returned to his face. He sang hymns with his family; the sound of his favorite, "Go Tell it on the Mountain," filled up the white halls of the hospital.

He joked and recalled memories, laughed and cried, hugged and held. Erik spoke to each of his brothers, willing specific belongings to each, and he recalled some of the summers spent with his family at Big Lake. For so long Erik had needed every bit of strength just to form a whisper, but on the night he died, Erik left nothing unsaid. In full voice he said his good-byes; he said his "I love yous"; he made his mom, dad, and brothers put their hands together on his chest and promise "to go on living and having fun."

Then, when he was good and ready, Erik looked at his mother, who was lying beside him on his hospital bed, and said, "If it's okay with you, I'm going to go now."

"It's okay, son," Sheri answered. "We love you, Erik."

Erik spread his arms, lifted his palms toward heaven, looked up at the sky, and, in an instant, was gone. An instant later, his hands went limp and his body was lifeless.

In the last moments of Erik's life, he didn't fight for a single breath, and he didn't feel one degree of fear. With the same grace Erik tackled his life, his fight, and his friendships, he also tackled death.

I got my miracle. It wasn't the miracle I'd imagined, but it was the one God had planned and delivered. Erik's passing was nothing less than miraculous. It challenged

Death Came to Stay

the laws of science and defied his disease. A boy who'd struggled to speak had said what he wanted to say. A teen-ager who'd struggled to breathe had filled his lungs with song. A young man who'd struggled to even walk, painlessly strolled into eternity.

You're gonna make it...

The last words Erik whispered to me hung in the air. What a contrast our two families had become. Brought together, a friendship made by two sons fighting the same disease. Similar veins, drugs, protocol, and the same faith stuck to the lives of both. Yet one boy's family received good news, as the other's was slapped across the face by loss. How could Erik's family not wonder why I was allowed to live every time they saw me? They wouldn't get to watch Erik graduate, marry, or hold his children. He was gone. Me being alive, getting good news at the very time Erik died, set off feelings of shame and made the grief I felt from my friend's death even worse.

There was reason for me to celebrate after surgery. It went well, and I was one step closer to surviving cancer. But when comparing my surgery's success to Erik's death and his family's heartbreak—I grieved. The deeper the grief was driven into me, the less significant my surgery became. Not only did emotion arising from Erik's death overpower the good news I'd been given, the surgery and the good news itself seemed passing: a silly, fading hope—a short-term grip on health that only pushed my life's question marks back one more day. There was no certainty in life, not for me or anyone else.

Death busted in. It showed up without an invitation and it came to stay. It took Erik. Tomorrow it might take the boy in the hospital bed across or next to mine, or Chad, or it could take me. The hospital constantly reminded me of grief, doubt, fear, and I didn't want to be at Children's for a second longer. I was supposed to be in the hospital for three weeks following the allograft, a thought that I couldn't bear.

I choked back tears as I stared at my doctor and asked, "What can I do to get out of here, Chappie?" I refused to look away until he answered.

Chappie closed my chart and pushed his glasses up the bridge of his nose. I suspect he knew why I wanted to leave so soon. Erik had been his friend, too. He thought about my question, and then he told me exactly what I'd have to do.

"Well, Jason, you'll need to keep food and fluids down without throwing up any portion of them. And you'll need to be completely off of any kind of strong pain medication for a few days."

"I'll do it!" I said.

When Chappie left the room, he took my morphine pump with him. I locked away emotion and fixed the same expression on my face for the rest of my time in the hospital. No matter how much my bones hurt or how sick I felt, I didn't allow my body to vomit or my face to reveal my pain.

Chappie visited me each evening, telling me, "Keep it up." Each evening after he left, I prayed with all my heart that I could. A three-week hospital stay shrank down to three days. By the time I was discharged, I'd become used to making due with a sawed, bolted, and stitched shoulder using only Tylenol as a painkiller.

On the way out of the hospital, I pulled the brake on my wheelchair. Dad and I stopped outside of Erik's room. It was nearly empty. The posters were gone, the red couch was gone, and Erik was gone. A nurse was alone in the room making up a vacant bed.

    I guess time had to keep pushing forward, forcing me to take the next step fighting cancer, forcing Rick and Sheri to live life without their son, and forcing doctors and nurses to go on caring for other sick people. Clock hands kept on ticking. Not even the death of my great and gracious friend could stop time from marching on. Suns kept on rising and seasons kept on turning.

    "Are you alright, son?" Dad asked.

    "Yeah, Dad."

    He unbuckled the brake on my wheelchair and pushed me forward.

Chapter Twenty-Two

Communion of Suffering

I knew all kinds of church words. Since before I could even talk, I'd learned about sin, repentance, grace, and redemption. But "communion" is the one that came to mind after Erik's death. It wasn't actually having bread and wine at church on Sunday that hit me; it's what it meant, the idea of suffering bringing people closer for some reason. And believe me, there's a communion when you're suffering next to somebody. As Erik and I suffered together, our friendship began, and in the same way after he died, his friends and family were heartbroken, and we joined together in a celebration of his life.

There was only room to stand in the church on the day of Erik's memorial service. People filled the pews, aisles, and the church's lobby. Each person cared for Erik in their own way; Erik's influence on each life was one of a kind. Each hurt differently, but on some level a broken heart is a broken heart. We were all connected by the same loss.

Blood relatives and near strangers came together, exchanging memories that made all miss Erik, and feel the pain from the missing. People gathered, and the grief they shared broke right into people's hearts, creating a deep and genuine bond among them. Erik was taken from all of us for the rest of our lives on earth, but a communion with those he left behind brought each close enough to reach out and say good-bye.

But I refused to be a part of it. I sat silent when people in the church sang "Go Tell it on the Mountain." My expression was fixed when others smiled at stories of Erik's grace. And I was cold, without tears, when people around me wept after hearing the story of Erik's miraculous death.

I couldn't understand any of this. It was unclear what I should be thinking or feeling, so I shoved everything aside. I leaned on a prideful will that covered my face with the same expression I'd practiced in the hospital after my allograft. I watched and listened, but stayed distant, closed up. All feeling was locked away. I just wanted the service to end.

As he was closing, Erik's pastor pointed out Chad, me, and another girl that I'd never seen at Children's. Her name was Jesse. The pastor prayed for kids everywhere fighting cancer. Then he prayed for the cancer in Chad's and my bodies, and for the cancer in Jesse's brain. Everyone sang, the pastor did a benediction, and the church was let out row by row. I watched Rick and Sheri pass by. Then Chad and Cherié. Finally Jesse passed by me.

So that's the girl Erik's pastor was talking about, I thought. *Hmm, Jesse, well maybe I'll meet her some other time. Not today. I'm getting out of this funeral fast as I can today.*

When our row was dismissed, I stepped into the center aisle and walked toward the back of the church. At the end of the aisle waiting for me, I was surprised to find Diane, my nurse from Children's. She reached out and wrapped her arms around me. I was stiff. I just wanted to walk past her, to get away from her hug and go home, but she kept holding me tight. Then something inside me cracked open. I stopped wanting to walk past, stopped trying to run from all that was happening. I melted into her embrace. My fixed expression, my mask, crumpled and tears began to flood. For the first time since the beginning of my treatment, I sobbed.

Stored-up tears poured down my face and soaked Diane's blouse. I gave up trying to control emotions that'd been screaming to surface. My friend was gone. I'd said nothing to Erik when I had the chance, because I didn't want to let him go. I wanted to hold on to him and the idea that life was fair, that Chad, Erik, and I would each be okay, that we'd grow up and that someday we'd look back and joke about this time. I realized that alongside all these people at the memorial service, this was my second chance to let go, to say what I should've said while sitting beside Erik in his hospital room—good-bye. I'd miss Erik forever, but letting go allowed my broken heart to begin to mend.

With red eyes and wet cheeks I spoke with a few of Erik's other friends and some of his family after the service. More stories were shared about Erik and cancer, and Erik before cancer.

It was there in the church's lobby that I first talked to Jesse.

As she walked past me, she said, "Hello, Jason."

Jesse smiled, not a grin or a smirk, but a downright smile. It was the sort you see on toothpaste commercials, white teeth and all. She was just a little shorter than me, but was bald just the same. Her head was partially covered up by a hat; if you looked around the edges it was easy to tell she didn't have hair, but I don't think it was meant to fool anybody. The hat just went along with her dress. She seemed elegant, bald head or not. I fumbled for something to say, while she calmly moved across the lobby, telling me "Hello" like it was nothing.

Looking at her bashfully, her smile drowning out the rest, I wiped away tears and tried to hide that I'd been crying. "Hi," I finally managed.

Though the conversation was just a word or two, I knew without a doubt, like Erik, there was a grace about her.

As Jesse passed by, I thought of her, Chad, and Erik, and I thought of all the other people who attended his service. I figured they were all thinking like I was.

Communion of Suffering

If a kid can die, no one else is off the hook when it comes to death. Like my dad told me, "Tomorrow is promised to neither sick nor the healthy, young nor old."

Sure, tragedy waits for everybody, but where do you go when statistics are no longer on your side?

Erik's pastor had pointed out us three cancer kids, three who needed prayer. There were many in the church who'd known Erik for longer, and were closer to him than Chad, Jesse, and I. But none seemed closer to their own funerals than the three of us.

Yes, I was scared of dying at times, and when that fear set in, I could think of nothing else. But the fear of losing my own life wasn't what made my gut wrench on the ride home from Erik's memorial—I was afraid of losing another friend. I was scared Chad might be next.

* * * * *

A Look Back: Life Abundantly

I did not compare cancer to fighting a deadly opponent. It was a fight to be sure, but more like being in a storm and having to battle from beginning to end to survive. Cancer filled my world—rolled over me—and I felt as though I was fighting to get through something, rather than combating it directly.

The days leading up to my diagnosis with Ewing's Sarcoma were like standing on a front porch alone, as a sky grows dark, trees start to sway, and small whirlwinds pick up grass clippings and leaves, carrying them down an empty street. The fair weather of health and happiness I enjoyed as a child was disturbed by the swirling winds of doctor's appointments, tests, scans, and surgeries. Dark clouds slowly moved in above me in the form of cancer, and the first raindrops came when I began chemotherapy. A distant thunder made me tremble as I witnessed suffering and contemplated mortality.

While fighting cancer I also encountered another storm, which was not terrible but was unstoppable, untamable; something I would eventually confront alone, apart from friends and family. I had been pushed to the brink of discovering faith.

The foundation of my faith lay in Judeo-Christian values, and particularly in the life, crucifixion, and resurrection of Jesus. I had known about faith all of my life, but it became real and intimate as I fought cancer. In the midst of difficulty and grief, something magical happened, something deep inside of me came alive.

A real encounter with faith is like the first gasp after a lifetime of restrained breath, the beginning of a divine respiration that awakens the senses to an all-new passion of skin and heart, thought, and desire. Faith is the craving for profound experience.

I have sometimes misunderstood this craving. Once discovered, faith ordained me with a desire to live wildly and, on occasion, this desire has been misguided. However, it has also urged me to risk, love, sacrifice, and long for abundant living. It is when I return my heart and desires entirely to God that I truly experience the profound, and capture that "life and life abundantly" that is promised in John 10:10.

Faith is not just experienced in Sunday morning sermons. It is not a boring set of rules. Rather, it is the crying from inside the soul to plunge into living. It is the cry from the sea: "Sail!" The cry from the mountain: "Climb!" And the cry from a starry night: "Wish!" It in-

spires childlike wonder and has escorted me through the colder, grayer mysteries of life. As I grow older, it is faith that convicts me of simple right and wrong, and labors to eliminate compromise and justification.

Like love, faith is born directly from God and thus does not follow the world's laws; it stirs the soul in such a way that it cannot be taken by death. I had seen suffering and mortality in Erik's circumstances, and his reaction to those circumstances pushed me to the edge of experiencing faith's first awakening breath.

* * * * *

Erik, Chad, and I had been in a battle where there was nowhere to turn, and no chance to really get away; we were stuck and stuck together. Fighting cancer, suffering through the same tough problems, caused the three of us to be closer than you could've imagined in such a short time, a closeness that made the empty space when Erik was gone that much greater. Erik's absence forced Chad and me to depend on each other that much more. After Erik's death, and because of Erik's death, Chad became the best friend I'd ever known.

We didn't have long conversations about Erik or his memorial service. Chad and I didn't talk our way through grief or about our feelings. He quietly walked me back to our van after the service.

"See you back at the house, Jay," he said.

We didn't talk about death, not Erik's, Chad's, or my own; there were some things Chad and I simply understood. A lot of people gave me advice and sent me books, but we didn't work through the "Five Steps of Grief"; there were no bullet points that could fix us. Still, the weeks after Erik died were a time of healing. Chad taught me to heal by remembering what it's like to be alive. In Chad I witnessed a charge on life, and from the depths of this charge, I heard a cry—a scream to live sincerely, to make every day mean something.

After Erik died, Chad was a picture of what it was to feel urgency in life. Chad was guaranteed nothing, not a clean bill of health, another birthday, a week, a day. The past and future only shared common ground, right now, in the present, and he refused to let even one moment pass without appreciating it.

He charged, but only softly. He screamed, but subtly. He showed me that we were surrounded by the extraordinary, but in the most ordinary way. Chad didn't look for daring thrills or spend lots of money. He simply enjoyed all the tiny gifts that he found in every single day. Chad didn't let a sensation go unnoticed, nor emotion slip by. It was a laugh at a joke, a stomp to a favorite song, the cool of grass and the warmth of a campfire, the sweetness of chocolate ice cream, and a cannonball into the deep end of a swimming pool. It was appreciating everyone who enjoyed those same things alongside of him.

Chad's charge took lungs full of breath and a heart that used every beat. It was a rush of how life should be lived. Following Erik's death, I truly believe that Chad was living for two.

Chapter Twenty-Three

Boys' Bathrooms Aren't Pink

After Erik died, I had nightmares, bad dreams about relapsing, and almost every night. There was one in particular I just couldn't shake, the same stupid dream over and over: a bone scan showing more cancer. It didn't matter how often I was in that exact nightmare, my stomach sank like it was the first time.

A large metal disc was attached to a mechanical arm. The arm slowly moved the disc up and down my body. I lay strapped to a long, thin table. The disc moved from my feet to my head, then back again. By the second pass, an image of my bones would be projected on a screen at the end of the long table.

If the screen showed a normal skeleton, the test was clear. If there was a bright dot on the screen attached to my arms or legs, my skull or my shoulder, it meant I had another tumor.

The disc completed its final pass, and I stared at the radiologist because my view of the screen was blocked: her face dropped, she saw something. The radiologist's concern made me afraid.

When finally able to see the screen—there were spots on my shoulder and skull. My cancer had relapsed and all hope for a cure was gone. The cancer would continue to spread and I would soon die.

* * * * *

"Jason...Jason!" Mom was gently shaking me.

I opened my eyes.
"It was a bad dream, Jason."
I wiped cold sweat from my face and sat up. The nightmare had been so real, I'd forgotten where I was. I looked out the window, at my yard, my street, my neighborhood.
"Whew," I said, glad the nightmare wasn't real, "what a relief."

"You don't have to go today. Do you want to wait until tomorrow?" Mom asked.

Rubbing my eyes, I answered, "No, Mom, I'll go today."

I was spending autumn at home, having some chemotherapy treatments at Saint Patrick's Hospital in Missoula. I'd missed the first week of sixth grade because I was in the hospital for a three-day chemotherapy treatment, and by now I actually wanted to go to school. When my energy and blood counts recovered between treatments, Dr. Speckart as well as Chappie and Dr. Pendergrass encouraged me to be in class with the other kids in Missoula. I looked forward to seeing my friends and going to a new school.

This year I would no longer go to the building where I'd attended kindergarten through fifth grade. I moved on to sixth grade at the middle school. Many of the other students had been in my classes every year since kindergarten, but I was very much the new kid. I had no idea who was going to recognize me, how the other students were going to react to my looks, or to the changes in me that so extremely affected my appearance and life.

Dad always took Jon and me to breakfast before the first day of school. He had offered to take my brother to breakfast a week before, on his first day, but Jon didn't want to go without me.

"Just wouldn't be the same," he'd said.

So on my first day of school, the three of us went together. We each ordered our traditional French toast and orange juice. We always ran late on the first day, so we ordered and ate fast, trying to get to school before the last bell.

We hurried down breakfast and then Dad sped to drop us off. I was actually early when I walked through the doors of my new school. I sat on a bench in the hallway while my father told the secretary at the office it was my first day.

"Your teacher will be right down," Dad told me.

Looking up, I took a deep breath and said, "I can handle this, Dad."

"Are you sure, son? I don't mind staying."

I nodded, "Yeah, this is nothin'."

"Pick you up at three o'clock then?" he asked.

"Nah, I'll walk home."

"Well, study hard."

I took a seat in the office and waited for my teacher. A few students passed by and waved at me. I waved back. A group of older girls walked by the office, looked at me, and began to whisper.

"Are you Jason?" one of the girls said.

"Yes," I answered—blushing.

They giggled and waved at me as they walked off.

"The kids have been looking forward to meeting you," said a woman now leaning against the door of the school's office.

"Really?" I asked, surprised.

"I will be your teacher this year," she said with a smile. She was blonde and pretty. I bet lots of guys my age would have a crush on her before long. "Would you like to see your new school?"

"Yes, m'am," I replied.

Boys' Bathrooms Aren't Pink

My teacher walked me to the classroom, giving me a tour of my new school on the way. She showed me the library and gymnasium, the playground, and lunchroom. It was much bigger than my old school.

"And here is our classroom," she said.

"Excuse me," I said, "but where're the bathrooms?"

She pointed, "They're right around the corner—"

Walking away from her and toward the bathroom, I tried not to make my urgent need too obvious. It'd only be seconds before I puked.

I turned the corner and ran into the bathroom, but couldn't make it to the toilet. My hand covered my mouth and held the vomit in until I could lean over a circular sink in the center of the room. I puked in the sink. The French toast and orange juice didn't taste as good coming up as they did going down.

In the midst of my coughing and spitting, I heard the school bell ring, and the other students rushed through the school's doors outside of the bathroom. My teacher did her best to help me dodge embarrassment. She stood outside the bathroom, guarding the door, not allowing anyone in.

I turned on the sink, cupped my hands, and splashed water on my face. Taking a deep breath, I looked around—*strange. My new school doesn't have urinals in the boy's bathroom.* I leaned over the faucet and rinsed my mouth. I again looked around—*this school really is nice; the boy's bathroom is way cleaner than at my last school.* Leaning over the faucet again, I took a drink. I swallowed—*I wonder why everything's pink in here.*

Straightening my shirt and putting on my cap, I held my head up and got ready to meet my new classmates. As I walked out of the bathroom, I found my teacher standing in front of a crowd of students explaining something to them.

She turned and opened her mouth, but nothing came out. It was clear she wasn't sure what to say. By the look on her face, you might've thought she was the one who'd thrown up in the girl's bathroom on the first day of sixth grade.

Chapter Twenty-Four

Fought the Good Fight, Finished the Race, Kept the Faith

Autumn leaves covered the ground and color erupted in Missoula's treetops. Walking home from school, I kicked through leaves that had fallen on the sidewalk. I'd become familiar with the sixth grade, and with the walk, as I was well enough to spend time with both in the past weeks. Sadly, when I turned our corner and saw Mom standing on the front steps, the look on her face was also familiar. I'd seen it twice before: when the doctors told me I had cancer, and when she told me Erik was dead.

Maybe you've seen it, too. It's the look of complete loss. The instant I saw her outside in the cold air, I knew she was waiting to tell me bad news. She fought to keep back her tears, but couldn't. Once I started up the narrow walk to our front door, she lost it. Like the last brittle leaf waiting to leave an empty tree, Mom's shaking hand covered her mouth.

Tears filled her eyes and she searched for the words. But there weren't any, and I already knew anyway. A dreaded fear was now real—cancer was taking another from our lives.

When the call came, Mom, Dad, Jon, and I left for Seattle right away. An all-night drive took us from our front door to the door of a hospital room at Children's. Inside, he sat on the bed, legs swinging just above the ground. It was a scene similar to the first time we met, except that I hardly recognized him.

Chemotherapy had been stopped because it wasn't working, allowing his eyelashes and eyebrows to begin growing. Different drugs had been started, including steroids and painkillers that had caused him to retain water and buried more weight beneath his skin than I thought possible. In both the hair and the weight I could see our doctors shrugging and shaking their heads, not knowing how to fight his relapsed tumors.

"Hey, Chad," I said, "How's it going?"

He rubbed his eyes and looked at the ground.

"I'm having a bad hair day, Jay," he said.

I laughed. Never did I really know what to say back to him. Chad grinned, as he did when pleased by a joke.

There he was. There was my friend. When the healthy heart and sense of humor hidden by cancer came out, Chad was easy to recognize.

"Let's get outta here," he said.

"Let's go!" I agreed.

I pushed Chad's wheelchair around the city on those final days, which included concerts and carnival rides. There were football games, movie tickets, and, of course, meals of ribs and mud pie split down the middle. There were no tears. No one feeling sorry for themselves. No running from the death waiting to strike at any moment, and there was no taking anything for granted until that moment showed up.

We bought these identical shirts with a picture of the two of us standing shoulder to shoulder. It was Chad's idea. And it was kind of a joke at first, doing something silly, funny, that'd be normal for nine-year-old girls at the mall—but I'm sure glad we got that picture and bought the shirts. Our smiles were forced, like our parents made us take the picture, or maybe somewhere deep inside we knew it'd be the last image of us together before Chad died. The picture was printed on two white T-shirts, along with the caption, *Best Friends*.

* * * * *

A Look Back: Boat to Eternity

My dad sometimes told a story about a young boy who had lost someone very close to him. After a tear-filled memorial service, the young boy was exhausted and fell asleep on a relative's floor. He began to dream.

He stood on a dock with his family, and in front of them sat a large ship. It was bigger and more beautiful than anything he had ever seen. Someone very close to him was aboard the ship waving good-bye. There were also many other families on the dock waving good-bye to people who were very close to them.

Some cried, some looked angry, and others just stared off into the distance. No one knew exactly where the ship was going to land, but everyone knew the journey and the destination would be extraordinary.

As the ship began to leave port, everyone on the dock was sad; they would not see their loved ones again until it was their turn to ride on the ship. The crowd watched the ship until it sailed out of sight. Once it was gone, all at once, sadness and anger were replaced by a feeling of peace. The crowd felt peaceful because they realized something: though they were sad, there was another crowd of people on the other side of the ocean waiting to welcome their loved ones with open arms.

When the boy awoke, he was not on the floor, but in his own warm bed. He did not know exactly how he got there, only that someone who loved him very much had scooped him up and carried him home. He smiled, realizing this was how his loved one felt—in a new place, not exactly sure how, but very sure it was home.

Fought the Good Fight, Finished the Race, Kept the Faith

* * * * *

At the end of Chad's life, there were certain things my best friend would allow, and certain things he would not. His humor was intact. His ability to persuade laughter when a laugh seemed out of the question stayed with him.

He wouldn't budge on a few other things either: he wouldn't give up the television controller. And he wouldn't give up his right to travel, on his own terms, to the bathroom—Chad wasn't going to die with a catheter. Doctors and nurses, his mother and friends, all tried to persuade Chad to reconsider, as his pain when moving was clear. Even so, he wouldn't give this up.

Rising slowly, he plodded to the bathroom, and when pain snatched his breath from him, he'd answer the gasps in the room, or someone trying to convince him to get a catheter with only one statement.

"I'm a new machine!" he'd exclaim, while bending his arms and flexing his biceps.

I spent days in a seat next to his bed. Chad's eyes were closed much of the time. When they did open, he managed some sort of remark. "You still here?" he'd ask. "Glad to see you sitting there, Jay. Reminds me I'm still alive—the angels gotta be better looking than you."

Each day I sat, the wisecracks drew further and further apart. His eyes remained closed more and more.

One night Rick and Sheri also came to the hospital to see Chad. During their visit, my father leaned over Chad's bed and asked, "Can I get you anything, Chad?"

He looked at Rick and Sheri, then at Dad, and he replied, "I'm not exactly sure what's gonna happen…ya know…when I go?"

His voice didn't falter and he didn't cry, but Chad was afraid. Death was taking him and he knew it. He didn't know what exactly to expect, or how bad it'd hurt.

Dad held Chad's hand in both of his and knelt by the hospital bed. When he and Chad were eye to eye, Dad began to tell Chad his story about the boy who fell asleep and dreamt of a ship leaving one port and arriving at another. He described the sadness of those waving good-bye to the ship, and he spoke of the joy felt by those greeting it on the other side. He told Chad that the boy woke up in his own bed; he wasn't sure how he got there, he didn't know much at all, except to say it was home.

When Dad finished telling the story, Chad pulled the blankets up to his chin.

"I get it," he said.

There was a long pause and then Chad asked, "Well, Reverend…would you pray for me?"

"Yes." Dad's voice quivered.

Chad's eyes were dry, but Dad's were not. He caught his breath and wiped a tear, then Dad took a step back. Chad held my left hand and Dad held my right, and a circle continued around Chad's bed: my mother, Sheri, Rick, and Cherié, who held Chad's other hand. Dad led everyone in the prayer from Matthew 6:9.

He began, and the rest followed:
Our Father, who art in heaven, hallowed be Thy name
Thy kingdom come, Thy will be done, on earth as it is in heaven…
Amen.

"Thanks, man." Chad said.

He took a deep breath and closed his eyes.

There was silence.

A ringing telephone reopened them.

He looked over at Cherié and asked with a touch of sarcasm, "Who could be calling at a time like this?"

Cherié picked up the phone, "Hello? Oh, we're hanging in there, and how're you?" She paused and looked at her son. "Just one moment, please. Chad? It's Paul Newman."

Paul Newman and Chad had become friends at Newman's "Hole in the Wall Gang" camp that summer. It was at camp when Chad found a bump on his arm. He was taken to the hospital, where the bump was diagnosed as another relapsed tumor. Paul Newman had spent a load of time with him after the tumor was found. He'd heard of Chad's worsening condition and here he was, calling to check on him.

None of us could keep from eavesdropping, and everyone in the room leaned a curious ear toward Chad's conversation. Most of the conversation consisted of, "Ah-huh's" and "Sure," "Yes," "No," and "Thank you." But when Paul Newman asked how Chad really was, if he believed that he was going to make it, Chad shot him straight.

"Well, Paul, I've been talking to my friend's dad here in the hospital and finally figured it all out," he said, winking and nodding at Dad. "It's like the spaghetti has just been hanging, waiting to fall, and it's finally hit the plate."

Were his words something profound or just a joke? Beats me. I was just holding on to every second I spent next to Chad's bed, to every word, confusing or otherwise.

I dove headlong into the reality of losing Chad, and into the fact that the time spent with him was precious. There was no prideful will or running from emotion. When emotion welled up and spilled over, I cried. When out of nowhere I felt like smiling, I smiled. When a look in Chad's eyes told me it was good-bye, I said good-bye.

"You know you're the best friend I ever had, Jay," Chad said.

"Yeah, you're my best friend, too, Chad."

"You know I'm not gonna see you for a long time?"

I nodded. "Yeah, I know."

"Man, I'm sure going to miss ya, Jay," Chad said.

"Well, I'm going to miss you, too, ya know," I answered, a little defensive.

Chad grinned.

I rested my head on the place where all of my questions, fears, anxieties, and hopes had lain ever since I'd started this fight, and Chad came into my life; I placed my head on his shoulder.

"I don't want you to go. I don't understa—"

"Wait a second," Chad interrupted. "It's like the Three Musketeers, and two of us will be there waiting. You know, Jay? Me and Erik will be waiting there for you."

I nodded.

"Chad?" I said.

"Yeah?" he answered.

Tears blurred my eyes, but I didn't look away.

"Good-bye, Chad," I whispered.

When Chad answered, I saw tears fill his eyes for the first time, "Good-bye, Jay."

I wrapped my arms around him and pulled my friend close one last time.

"I'll be watching for you, Jay," he whispered.

I slowly let go of Chad.

Leaving his hospital room, I didn't turn around or look back until I was outside of Children's.

Outside, it was raining hard, the kind of sopping Seattle rain that made the people around here wear long coats and carry dark umbrellas. I didn't have a raincoat or an umbrella as I started walking toward the McDonald House. Raindrops and teardrops mixed until I didn't know which was which. I was alone. Three of us friends had become only two, and now I was by myself.

With what felt like long, cold fingers, terror was massaged into my skin. The fact that my allograft and treatments were going well meant nothing. Watching cancer steal life from my friends was more real than good news from doctors. I no longer believed that I had a strong hold on surviving cancer. I believed instead that I barely held onto life; I was just waiting for it to slip through my fingers.

I'd never been so alone. I'd never been so sad. I'd never been so afraid. At rock bottom and with nothing left to hold on to, something startling happened. In a cold, hopeless surrender, I rested everything on my faith. There was nothing else.

Standing in the rain, alone, soaking wet and weeping, faith truly awakened inside of me. I was overcome by a clarity that God knew me, cared for me, and stood beside me—a feeling that somehow God and I had a deep and very real friendship. I was overcome by a belief that faith in God wouldn't make life easy, but it would give me strength and joy even in the middle of the toughest times possible. And like my friends before me, I believed wholeheartedly in a promise: when I died, I'd go to heaven with Erik and Chad.

That feeling of closeness stayed right with me every day, but I still cried my eyes out when Chad died. I think it was the saddest day of my whole life.

Chad's death was different than Erik's. Chad didn't sing hymns or lift his palms towards heaven, and he didn't spread his arms and say good-bye in peace. Chad's knuckles were white and his teeth were gritting when he died. There was blood, and it was frightening. When you really think about it though, his death was no less miraculous than Erik's. You only see heaven for the first time, one time; and know how your tiny piece fits into a grand plan for the first time, one time.

The world tested Chad more than anyone I'd ever known. It hit him with the most difficult problems, and in the end he was made stronger. Chad ended his life in the same way he lived it. His determination never faded and his humor never failed.

The communion of suffering alongside Chad and Erik created strong friendship. And it was that same communion, after their deaths, which created true strength in my faith—it wasn't Dad's, it wasn't Erik's, it wasn't Chad's, but was my own. Courted by tragedy, I found my faith, and fell in love with life.

And so, I needed to fight. I was reminded of this by a verse that was part of Chad's and Erik's lives. It's found in 2 Timothy 4:7, and it's etched into each of their gravestones, and into my heart:

"I have fought the good fight, I have finished the race, I have kept the faith."

Chapter Twenty-Five

Traveling to Russia, Returning to Serve

After Chad's death, there was another returning nightmare that I just couldn't shake:

I'm walking along a narrow ledge. My trail is full of bumps and dips, and there is no moon, no stars, no light to guide me. The path is sturdy, and all I have to do is walk carefully, and watch my step.

It seems as if I've walked for a long time and I am beginning to feel experienced and sure in my footing, when my left foot falls upon an unexpected bump. I lose my balance and find myself falling.

I hit the ground terribly hard and began to slide down a steep hill. My slide is not extremely quick. Momentum is neither gained nor lost, and I slide steadily.

Looking down the hill, I can see that at its edge lies a cliff. The cliff approaches closer and closer, my eyes and mind tell my heart and bones that I will not survive the fall.

Reaching to my right and left, I try desperately to clutch a branch or a rock, anything that will stop me from sliding. But everything I reach for passes me by, or crumbles in my hands.

Sliding toward the cliff, no faster, but no slower, I can do nothing to stop my steady descent, but I cannot stop from trying. To no avail, I reach, I clutch, and I dig my heels into the ground.

I arrive at the cliff's edge. Barely gripping a ridge with my fingertips, I hang looking down at the fall that lies below. I brace myself for the fall, for death, and—

* * * * *

I woke up with a gasp. "It was just a dream, Jason, it was just a dream," I said out loud.

Wiping the sweat from my face, I got up and walked down the hall to get a glass of water from the kitchen.

My nightmares were so real and so often that nearly every night I had trouble sleeping. Nearly every night, I woke in a cold sweat. On these nights, I often walked to get a glass of water, and many times I'd see my father in his office as I passed.

The edge of Dad's desk and the border of his computer screen were lined with yellow sticky notes. The notes were reminders of some kind, scribbles really, that no one but Dad could understand. His desk was always cluttered despite his efforts to organize it. He sorted papers and returned books to their proper place on his shelves, but it seemed like they stacked up more quickly than he could put them away. Yet, there was always a space in the center of the desk cleared for Dad's Bible. The Bible was forever open, and there were papers with notations inside next to the pages, but the pages of the Bible were never marked.

For many years I believed that if I had a problem, all I needed to do to find a solution was lean over a Bible and rub my chin. That's how Dad solved all of our family's problems.

As expected, Dad was in his office reading when I passed, but on this night, tears streamed down his face. He showed me the letter he was reading. A church group was traveling to a newly liberated Russia; it'd be the first Christmas the Russian people were allowed to celebrate in over seventy years. Dad mostly cried at the good stuff. He was usually fine at funerals or if someone was fighting mad, but when it came to baptisms, baby dedications, weddings, and I guess kids getting their first Christmas present, he needed a hanky.

The group planned to give millions of dollars in medical supplies to hospitals, and Christmas gifts to all the children stuck in treatment there. Dad decided we were going with them to Moscow.

Family, friends, and our community supported us, making the trip possible for my parents, Jon, and me. It wasn't as easy to convince my doctors.

"You want to do what?" Dr. Speckart said. He shook his head. "Traveling to a country needing medical aid from the United States is not the place for a patient who's in need of constant medical attention. I can't believe this."

"Guess this would be a bad time to ask if I can play in my basketball game on Friday night?" I asked.

My red blood cells were awfully low, so it was difficult to get needed oxygen to my muscles and organs. My body was struggling to function, much less run up and down a basketball court. If overexerted, my heart could, almost literally, explode because it was working too hard.

I just wasn't the athlete I was before treatment. Chemo had damaged the muscles in my heart, joints, and ligaments, and stolen my reflexes. I became pigeon-toed as a result of treatment, and all the bounce I once had was replaced with a clumsy thump.

I'd need to take aspirin every period of the game to battle the pain from playing, and still, I'd be forced to spend much of my time on the bench. It didn't matter.

I wanted to play.

"What do you think?" I asked again.

Bald and bronzed on top, hair a little wild on the sides and back of his head, Dr. Speckart gave me a frank look through perfectly round eyeglasses, "Jason," He said, "there is a man down the hall who is going to die. His condition is such that if I give him the wrong medicine, or a little too much of the right medicine, I am going to kill him. Your approach to this disease makes you a more difficult patient than that man down the hall."

"Sooo...I guess that's a no," I said.

Dr. Speckart looked at my medical chart and again shook his head, "Yes...you can play in your basketball game. And if Chappie and Dr. Pendergrass also approve you can go to Russia."

Chappie and Dr. Pendergrass gave in to the idea of our family traveling to Moscow. And so, with no real agenda and no idea what to expect, we boarded a plane and headed halfway around the world.

* * * * *

A Look Back: The Joy of Knowing Outweighs the Pain of Losing

In Chad's and Erik's deaths there was a wound, in the wound there was a choice, and in the choice lay the difference between my fight with cancer and others'. I could have chosen to callous my heart. Or I could have chosen to open and offer it, despite knowing that caring for others—especially those fighting cancer—opened me to be wounded once again.

I calloused my heart and protected it from the torment of grief after Chad and Erik died. The trapeze art of loving and losing wore me down; I grew weary of opening my heart to anyone and let few close to me. Besides those friends with whom I fought cancer, it would be years before I truly cared for another child facing the disease.

During my biopsy in Missoula, treatments at Children's Hospital, and by the bedsides of Chad and Erik, a biblical story recurred in my dad's mind. He was reminded of a pool in Jerusalem where the diseased would lay, waiting for the waters to be divinely churned. Once churned, there was a race toward the moving waters, and the first to enter the pool was said to be healed. One man had spent thirty-eight years trying to enter the waters, but was never able to reach the pool first. John 5:1-8 tells of how Jesus came upon this man and asked him a peculiar question: "Do you want to get well?"

I had seen the innocent fight with soul and spirit until their final hour, but still their lives expired, and family and friends remained and grieved. I had prayed for miracles and asked a capable God to save those close to me. He did not, and again I felt grief. I don't know why some live and some die, nor am I sure why Jesus felt the need to ask an invalid who had dedicated thirty-eight years to the cause of healing if he wanted to get well. These are questions I am still living today.

I have conviction, however, that some of life is circumstantial and out of our hands, but much of life must be lived on purpose. In the biblical story, the invalid answered Jesus, demonstrating that he indeed wanted to be well and needed help. He deliberately chose to be healed of his ailment and was given health, a few more good years on earth. In his miracle he was also given faith, clarity to believe in the Jesus who healed him, and a more eternal perspective. When I get to heaven I want to find this man, and ask him a question.

"When you received the miracle, what was more important: the few good years given on earth following your healing, or the faith that remains throughout eternity?"

My dad has told me on several occasions that when a person is hurt on the outside, the heart and soul sometimes gain health inside—they may be conditioned for heaven while skin and bone, heartbeat and breath are taken. I have adopted this perspective. I believe that God's measure is far different from my earthly measure, his plan exceeds my finite understanding, and what I presently see as terrible may become perfection when viewed eternally.

I also believe that this perspective, or any perspective for that matter, falls short of erasing pain or healing broken hearts. Even if revelation was granted and God's plan could be understood in the moment a loved one died, I would miss them and my heart would remain broken. In the Christian faith, we believe Jesus had divine power and perspective, yet when his friend Lazarus died, he grieved—even for Jesus, there was pain with loss.

The death of a child is the greatest loss I have ever witnessed. I will never forget the weeping sound of a mother grieving, nor the deep, hollow sobs of a father. I can only guess at the grief felt by Chad's and Erik's parents. Every room in their homes, every season, birthday, and holiday would be different than before cancer stole their beloved children. There would always be memories of their child's life, so there would always be reminders of death. So what can Cherié, Sheri, and Rick look forward to? To their own deaths? To arriving at heaven's gates, when once again they will be reunited with Chad and Erik?

Things never return to the way they were before a tragedy. A heart is never fully restored following the death of a child. However, there is healing and abundant life after loss. I have felt a healing within myself, and I have witnessed a slow healing in the parents who said good-bye to their children inside of the Hospital. There is a day when the joy of knowing outweighs the pain of losing.

In the bitter-sweet intoxication of missing, the hangover and sickness come first. When the wound of letting go is fresh, grief overwhelms—despair heats up inside, sorrow builds, and eventually boils into a fever. Although grief may never totally disappear, time passes, and a year arrives when a birthday can be enjoyed and a holiday celebrated. There is a moment when the fever breaks and joy arising from memories of days spent with a loved one outweighs the pain from losing them.

It is then that life is no longer a tragedy, but becomes a romance once again. When life is again a romance, there is a realization that caring for more than oneself is a paradox that provokes a heart to be broken, but at the same time, also touches life and makes it beautiful and extraordinary.

Like the invalid from the Bible story, I wasn't given the choice of whether or not I would suffer from disease. I was born, grew older, and became sick. Cancer paid no mind to my wants or desires. However, I fought cancer on purpose. I believed and had faith on purpose. When I first prayed for Erik, I deliberately ventured beyond my own disease and began to truly care about someone else's health. This continued on to Chad and onward again; years after my disease was gone, I began to care for other children in the thick of their own fight.

Mother Theresa instructed, "Love until it hurts." When there is hurt, when loving costs something, maybe this makes love selfless, makes us appreciate the moments we share with each other all the more. Caring for friends fighting cancer was reckless and has left me deeply

Traveling to Russia, Returning to Serve

wounded. But true to the paradox, these friendships have provided me with unexpected beauty, like fireworks lighting up an ordinary night. And I would not trade that for ease or an unbroken heart. Like living my questions, I dwell in the hope and belief that the day will come when heartbreak lessens and answers become clear.

* * * * *

I sat alone in our Moscow hotel room. Out the window, snow fell from a cloudy sky onto barren trees and slushy streets. The colors of Russia's architecture were all the more striking in the dead of winter. Like huge candy-cane teardrops, or exotic twists of whipped cream topping a big birthday cake, the swirling red and green, golden and blue peaks of Saint Basil's Cathedral caught my eye. Next to the cathedral, several giant lights shone brightly on Red Square and the Kremlin. At the foot of each structure gathered a mob, a crowd of angry people protesting their new government, wanting the country to be Communist again.

Looking to the floor of the hotel room, I noticed a box lying at my feet. It was filled with a number of small toys. Picking up a package of four toy cars, I looked at them, and then back out the window at the mob. I tried to open the package, but my hands began to shake, then my arms and torso. I dropped the package, pulled the blanket from the hotel bed, wrapped it around me, and curled up on the floor. Thoughts of the pediatric cancer wards I'd visited in Russia made my body quake.

I recalled walking down the concrete stairs of a hospital, between the cold gray cinder block walls, into what I felt must be a basement. I remembered my surprise when I found this basement was the place where children with cancer were treated.

Far away from home, I was again next to kids fighting cancer. The children in these hospitals had the same disease as I did, though they didn't receive the same treatment. Few of the children were completely bald. Some had thinned hair, some had bald patches, others looked normal despite the tubes running from their bodies. I remembered Chad's regrowth of hair; in these children I could also see doctors shrugging and shaking their heads, not knowing how to fight the relapsing tumors, or lacking the tools to do so.

The same needles were used again and again on different patients. IVs ran from veins in the children's arms and feet, and I could see burns on their skin from spilling chemo. They didn't have the good fortune of a Port-a-cath.

Differences separating me from these children seemed vast: wider than when I only knew about real problems because of the news, or when I still had a full head of hair and first saw someone sick with cancer, even more massive than the ocean we'd crossed to visit these kids. I stood next to the kids in Russia with my bald head, my Chicago Bulls cap, and the newest medical gadgets under my skin. I had experimental drugs in my veins, hundreds of thousands of dollars invested in my health. I had a fighting chance. By some other chance, the Russian kids were born in a place where they were given a feeble shot at treatment, but really, where they were sent to a basement to die.

To even all this out and tip the scales in their favor a bit, when I visited the children, I brought them a gift bag. In the bag was a set of clothes and a toy. The small gifts and even the medical supplies we brought to the hospitals all of a sudden didn't seem like much at all; just my being there seemed to insult people less fortunate than me. *How could I not remind the children and their parents how lucky I was? How could they not wonder why I was given treatment, hope, and they heartache and loss, and a slap in the face kind of like Erik's and Chad's families?* I don't know what exactly these children and their parents were thinking. But I can say, firsthand, even if they asked these questions, their actions said something different.

The scene didn't change much as I visited different hospitals. Russian children were put in a cold, cinder-block basement. Needles were used again and again. Skin was burned. Death—a promise. And at the end of every visit, after I spoke with the children through an interpreter and helped hand out their gift bags, a line would form.

In front of me, at each hospital we visited, child and parent stood in a line. Sometimes the lines were quite long, extending the entire length of the hallway in the Russian hospital. In the hand of each child there was a toy, often the same one we'd given to them for Christmas, and probably the only toy they'd receive. An interpreter relayed their gratitude.

"Thank you," said the child.

"Thank you" said some parents; "God bless," said others.

Some of them hugged me. Some of them shook my hand. All of the parents told me they were grateful, and all of the children offered the gift of a toy.

I didn't know what to do. Puzzled, I looked at Dad. *Should I accept?*

He nodded, and I accepted the children's gifts.

It seemed the gifts we'd brought them weren't important—still they were grateful. To me it seemed that I had everything and these people nothing—still they gave. This unexpected gratitude, even joy, was in no way based on belongings. They smiled because of a gift that was bigger than toys or clothes, but was wrapped around them, and was something much more than some prize that'd end up collecting dust in a toy box.

There was no question that faith brought my family to Russia, but we didn't come wanting to preaching at anyone, nor did we come expecting anything. As we'd done again and again in the past months, we stepped blindly forward. We trusted that where we were was just where we ought to be. We simply showed up, gave ourselves away, and hoped a hint of the faith that carried us through cancer and brought us to Moscow, could somehow be seen.

I didn't understand exactly why the kids there felt the need to give back to me. But looking at line after line of children and parents, in hospital after hospital, I started believing that when given selflessly, honestly, from down deep—faith is contagious.

There is something really beautiful in that spirit of communion. Sometimes without even one word, it brings people who are suffering in the same way closer to each other. It gives just a glimpse, just for a moment of something, well, Dad says, something holy. At first glance, the Russian kids and I seemed far apart. We weren't so different, though. We were part of a similar suffering—on some level a broken heart is a broken heart. A silent, but strangely close friendship broke through language barriers, politics, and even religion.

The memory of our experiences in Russia was powerful and left me curled up on the floor, my whole body trembling. Most would think the image of a sick child shriveled up on the floor of a hotel room, shaking with sadness and anger, isn't a picture of beauty. To an outsider it'd look pretty weird. But can you believe it was beautiful? Because, if you think about it, no matter how bad things get—a heart is made to beat, it's made to love, and if we choose to care about others, as sure as it'll beat, it'll break.

Chapter Twenty-Six

A Young Lady, Different from the Rest

I'd made it through summer, autumn, Christmas, and winter. Then spring came to Montana once again. It'd been almost one year exactly since my diagnosis with cancer. New life and color outside came along with new hope in my life. Each treatment, bone scan, and MRI that came back clear, brought me one step closer to surviving. But despite my growing hope, I don't think I ever really got away from thinking about death. Just like cancer, it was now always in the front or back of my mind.

After we buried Erik and Chad, I was allowed to stay home most of the time and have treatments at the hospital in Missoula. I'd almost entirely closed up, cut myself off from Children's Hospital and the McDonald House. Jesse was the only other kid fighting cancer that was close to me. I wasn't looking for new cancer friends. But our families spent so much time together that we didn't have much choice; in a way, Jesse and I had to be friends.

My very first talk with Jesse just after Erik's memorial was only a few words long, but I remembered her clear as day. She and I were about the same size and age. Her skin was white; a touch of freckles covered her cheeks and the bridge of her nose. Jesse's eyes were bright and blue. And that smile; it was the kind of smile you noticed right away, and missed when it went away.

Most of the girls at Children's wore wigs to cover their heads. Jesse didn't wear a wig, at least not to Erik's memorial. She wore a flowery hat that matched her pastel dress, not hiding but making the whole outfit, bald head and all, seem like it was just right. Sure she had cancer, anyone could see that. A small scar even let on that she had a brain tumor. Yet, Jesse was okay with her disease and the way she looked, which seemed to put everyone at ease. You noticed the girl far more than the sickness.

Jesse had walked past me in the church's lobby, toward a line of people who waited to say their condolences to Rick and Sheri and the rest of Erik's family. She caught up with her parents in the line. Her mom, Carol, was a tall, thin, blonde woman; Pat, her dad, had a thick jaw and shoulders.

She reached over to hold her mom's hand. I watched the line move up, and Jesse's mother and father hugged Rick and Sheri when it was their turn. Then Sheri bent down and held Jesse for what seemed like a long time. Rick did the same, and her small body and pastel dress nearly disappeared in his full grown arms and large suit coat.

Jesse found her way inside my life right then. At that moment we were pressed close by facing similar grief and disease. It wasn't long before our parents made sure to schedule check-ups together at Children's Hospital so we could see each other. Whenever we had to go to Washington, my family always visited Jesse, Pat, Carol, and Jesse's brother and sisters in Bellingham. Jesse's family made the long trip to Missoula, too. She kind of picked up where Erik left off when it came to me learning about grace. When Jesse stepped in, I just assumed God was telling me that there was patience and kindness I still didn't have. Even though Jesse and Erik both taught me how to be a bit more graceful, she affected me in another way, because she was a young lady and quite different from the rest.

I think she saw sickness, the planet earth, life, all of it, in her own unique way. I was a little bigger, and of course, thought I was much stronger than she, but sometimes Jesse could just walk in and make something happen with the gentlest touch; something that I'd been fiddling around with for quite awhile.

I remember the time when our family was visiting hers in Bellingham, and we were working on a jigsaw puzzle together. She talked softly, helping me without making it a big deal, "Just do this, Jason," she'd whispered, effortlessly pushing in a puzzle piece.

I knew the picture matched up, but I just couldn't fit it, I thought, "Thanks," I'd mumbled, bested but obliged to move on and look for the next match.

I was never exactly sure if she was glad we were mashed together by the same disease, but when it came down to it, Jesse always helped me out. Once she even walked with me to a bone scan at Children's Hospital and then waited with me afterward when it didn't go well.

Right away, I knew it was bad. I remember thinking, *Do the radiologists think they were fooling anyone? I've seen this stupid scan, this same outline of my skeleton a thousand times.* I was lying there, waiting for that big disk to scan up and down my body so I could peek at the results on a screen, hoping, praying there wouldn't be a big bright spot showing growth where there should be none. Joints, they've got to grow. Growth plates, too. For a kid, that's normal. But a spot in the middle of my rib, where I'd never seen a spot before, that's what you called a "hot spot."

When the radiologist said, "Excuse me for a minute," while leaving the room, that meant a specialist needed to carefully look at the hot spot. And that meant relapse.

The radiologist came back into the room later with an uneasy smile and finished the scan; the results wouldn't be given until I saw Dr. Pendergrass at Clinic hours later. But I knew.

The bone scan's giant disk slowly moved over my body once again, and the radiologist tilted a TV screen showing *The Little Mermaid* in my direction. My stomach sank, sick with nervousness, the fear of relapse, the memory of Chad and Erik dying. I'd never watch that cartoon again without feeling the same sickness, remembering the metal and alcohol smell of a bad bone scan.

When the scan was done, I took a deep breath. And when I was sure that I no

A Young Lady, Different from the Rest

longer looked terrified, I walked out to the waiting room. My family and a few other friends were sitting there. As soon as she laid eyes on me, Jesse, in a seat next to my mother, sat up straighter than before. It took one glance for her to figure out there was a problem.

"They saw something," I said quietly, sitting next to her silently, my head drooping.

I think we both jumped a little when Jesse touched my hand. But she did, and she left it there, recovering from the shock quicker than me—her hand stayed right on top of mine.

"Don't worry until you're sure there's something to worry about, Jason," always ending with—*Jason*. It's like there was no word left in the English dictionary when she said my name that way. She patted the top of my hand, and then slowly pulled away and folded both hands on her lap.

The hot spot turned out to be nothing, a bruise from roughhousing, lying on my side wrong during a five-day treatment. I don't know. But Dr. Pendergrass told me a few hours later that it wasn't serious and, as if the scan had never happened, hope of beating cancer fast returned.

Like me, there was also new hope for Jesse and her family that spring. Surgeries on Jesse's brain, her chemotherapy, and radiation treatments had worked. There was no sign of a brain tumor: she was cancer free! And there was more: Jesse had a brand new line of beauty products, soaps and lotions, and other things for girls. *Jesse's Perfect Peach* was sold at Nordstrom's stores, and money from the soaps and lotions went to Children's Hospital. The product line even won her the *Young Philanthropist of the Year* award. She was humble and so graceful when she got the award. Certainly I didn't care for fruity-smelling soap, but she raised close to sixty-thousand dollars for charity, so even I knew it was a big deal, and we were all really proud of her.

About that time, Make-A-Wish granted Jesse and me our wishes. Her wish was to have tea at the Four Seasons Hotel in Seattle. Make-A-Wish went well beyond her request and treated her and her friends to a whole weekend at the Four Seasons, lots of tea, and a shopping spree.

It's hard deciding on a wish. Think of asking for almost anything you wanted. When it came down to my wish, I tried to trick them and get a couple. … Vacation or meeting Michael Jordan? … Vacation? … Jordan? I kept going back and forth and finally combined the two—vacation *with* Michael Jordan!

My wish was to meet Michael Jordan at Disney World. I probably could've guessed that Jordan couldn't make it to our family vacation. I could've gone to see the Chicago Bulls play and maybe met him after the game, but I couldn't fault *The Little Mermaid* for being on TV when a radiologist found the "hot spot" on my rib. Once my family was given a formal invitation from Disney, I decided on visiting the Magic Kingdom in Orlando instead of a Bulls game.

Jesse was eleven years old, and I was twelve. You wouldn't need to look much further than our wishes to see the differences between boys and girls at our age. Dressing up, drinking tea, and going on shopping sprees made no sense to me; and the idea of professional sports, and looking up to someone whom I'd never met and knew almost nothing about seemed silly to Jesse.

With check-ups and holidays, Jesse and I saw each other often. It was usually only a few months from one time to the next, and sometimes there were just weeks between visits. Our parents talked on the phone, too, and not just our moms. Dad, Rick, and Pat had a sort of father friendship that sparked just about on the spot. Jesse and I didn't keep in touch like that, so it was exciting when we were in the same place. We'd hug each other, both of us a little on edge until the squeeze was over.

Sure, I was a boy and Jesse was a girl, but there was an even bigger difference between us. A long and hard fight against cancer had left Jesse with a maturity about two decades beyond my own. And while we were always truly happy to see each other, it never took long for Jesse to comment on my immaturity.

She didn't think it was funny when I splashed her in a pool or sprayed her with a hose. She was disgusted when I wiped my nose with the back of my hand, and she got downright angry when I hit her with a snowball when we were all together in Montana one Christmas.

"Be careful! You could've poked my eye out, Jason," Jesse said.

Always ending with—*Jason*. "I didn't even thinka that," was my skimpy defense, but it was all I could come up with after she tacked my name on at the end.

Another time we were all visiting Rick and Sheri at Big Lake, or what I called Erik's Lake. Hiding near the dock, I threw some small rocks, trying to flatten a sand castle that Jesse's younger brother and sister had built.

"Jason! Would you stop?" Jesse said, from a relaxed position on a lawn chair where she had been watching her siblings have fun. "Gosh," she sighed, "So annoying! Why's he always throwing things?"

I had a bunch of stones left, and had spent a while gathering them all up, but that was the end of it. "Sorry, Jesse," I gave in, halting my childish behavior.

You could argue that this boy and girl of the same age and similar families were distanced even further than children living oceans apart. The closeness between kids fighting the same disease stretched to its absolute limit for the two of us, but it was there. Jesse and I were at an age where we'd never admit it, but we totally supported each other.

Near the end of my fight with cancer, Jesse was someone I looked up to, a teacher—a close friend. She had wisdom that I simply didn't possess. I always wondered how she could be right all the time; she didn't just have *an* answer, she always seemed to have *the* answer.

I was there for Jesse, too, but what I gave to the friendship was simpler. I surprised her, and made her smile or laugh when she didn't want to. I was there to get a tangled kite from an out-of-reach tree limb, to hop a fence and unlatch a locked gate, and to accidentally spill soda on the pages of her favorite book. I was there to understand what it's like to be a kid with cancer when no one else could, and to push her on a tire swing.

* * * * *

A Look Back: Jesse and her Family

Pat and Carol first met at an Eastern Washington University school dance. A tall, bashful Carol took Pat's hand and he led her onto the dance floor. As the DJ played the 1974 hit, "Come and Get Your Love," by Redbone, Pat and Carol drew the attention of friends attending the dance, and today many of these friends concede that some things are meant to be.

The couple was married in Bellingham, Washington, on August 21, 1976. Jesse, their first

A Young Lady, Different from the Rest

child, was born in 1980, and they came home from the hospital in Pat's 1978 MGB. There was no car seat. There were no seat belts. Jesse was wrapped in a warm blanket, placed in a very nice wicker basket, and away they went.

Jesse did not cry much as an infant, and for the most part, she slept through the night. The couple assumed having kids was a breeze and decided to have more. Jesse's younger sisters, Lindsey and Kate followed, and just six weeks before Jesse was diagnosed with cancer, Pat and Carol had their first boy, Taylor.

Pat and Carol raised their children in a historic part of Bellingham. A park ran through the community of old houses mostly built in the 1920s and 1930s. When viewed from above, the park resembled a green ribbon lacing through the ripened neighborhood. It was a perfect neighborhood for a lemonade stand, and during her childhood, Jesse spent time sitting outside behind a table with a glass pitcher and sign that read, "LEMONADE 25 CENTS A CUP."

One day a customer asked to purchase a bouquet of flowers that Jesse had added to her lemonade stand for decoration. She agreed to sell the bouquet, and the customer filled Jesse's hand with quarters. Her eyes lit up, and from then on, she sold bouquets of flowers rather than cups of lemonade. Jesse's flower stand became an expected presence in the neighborhood during spring and summer.

Neighbors and passersby saw less of Jesse's flower stand following her diagnosis with a brain tumor in 1989. She was in and out of treatment for several years. The lives of Jesse and her family became exceedingly difficult in 1994 when she relapsed and a stem-cell transplant became her last hope for survival. At this time Jesse's mother was also diagnosed with cancer.

Carol, the tall and once bashful bride now faced breast cancer. Meanwhile her daughter, the infant she'd wrapped in a warm blanket and brought home in a very nice basket, had one final chance to make it through brain cancer.

Jesse and her mother were bald and too skinny to appear healthy. The two received second glances from strangers they referred to as "Staring Fans": foolish strangers who didn't understand the hurtful consequences of looking too long. As a parent and a Christian, the stares made Carol wonder if she could have done something different while raising her children. She not only endured her own cancer and the agony of watching Jesse suffer, she also lay awake at night in shame and guilt wondering if the pain in her family was somehow God's punishment. The physical struggle to survive cancer accompanied the greatest spiritual struggle of Carol's life.

I must've done something unforgivable for God to allow such a nightmare, for both my daughter and myself to have cancer at the same time, *Carol thought.*

The time Carol and Jesse spent together while fighting cancer was difficult and far from ideal. Still, it remains cherished. Carol had been stripped of many of the things she had known and valued throughout her life. She was no longer a blonde, a mastectomy had changed her figure, and cancer threatened both her life and the life of her daughter. Safety, emotion, religion, and glamour were undressed, and with nothing else to stand in the way—the relationship between Carol and Jesse flourished. Carol enjoyed a bond with her daughter that others could only dream of.

Carol began to understand how important it was to see God through Jesse's eyes.

"I'll be fine, Mommy...but give me a kiss just in case something happens...and it's time to go see Jesus," she told Carol.

Jesse's trust in the benevolent Jesus described in the Bible was unwavering. She did not believe Jesus looked at her and Carol with the coarse, punishing eyes of "Staring Fans." Rather, he looked at them with a loving gaze that had followed them both through every day of their lives: through their births, first steps, first words, Jesse's flower stand, and Carol's maternity.

In Jesse's charming, quiet way, she taught Carol about living deeply in the midst of their difficulty. She stopped her mother from trying to look from the outside to see how others perceived the two of them. And she introduced Carol to a Jesus who was interested in relationship much more than punishment.

I first met Jesse and her family in 1992, years before Carol's diagnosis. Jesse and I became friends towards the end of my battle with cancer, and so my memories with her have less to do with vomit and hospitals and more to do with figuring out "life after treatment." About the time I finished my last round of chemotherapy, Jesse was also enjoying a period in her life without cancer in her body. Our hair began growing back, grades and attendance at school began to seem important again, and when we felt nauseous, sometimes it was just the flu.

Again, in an event that would only later prove to be profound, on a trip to Seattle for one of my check-ups, Grandpa Greer met Jesse. Taken aback by her strength and faith, upon his return to Montana, he immediately made her a silver ring with the emblem of a fish on it. Except for being slighter and smaller for a young girl's hand, the ring was identical to the one he made for me when my family and I first traveled to Children's Hospital.

* * * * *

By August, my blood counts were too low—too low to fight off infection and even too low to have treatments most of the time. Chemo was being pushed back and back, because my body couldn't bounce back and repair red and white blood cells between treatments. I began fighting cancer in 1991, and Dr. Pendergrass told me treatment would last eighteen months. It was now 1992, late summer, about a year and a half since I'd been diagnosed—but treatment was at a standstill. *You gotta be kidding me, I'm never gonna finish.*

What I didn't know was that my doctors were making a tough decision: they could either stop chemotherapy for a few months, let me recover, and then begin again, or they could stop treatment for good.

I'd gotten used to having chemo at the hospital in Missoula, so I was surprised when Dr. Pendergrass wanted me to come back to Seattle for a treatment. I was even more surprised by what he told me in the examining room at Bone Tumor Clinic.

"I'm ready," I said. "Only four more to go—let's get 'em over with."

"Nope. Sorry, Jason," Dr. Pendergrass replied.

My heart sank, and I searched the doctor's face for a clue of what he might say next. *Did I need more treatment? Did I relapse?*

"Jason, your body can't take any more," he said. "This treatment will be your last."

It took a minute to sink in.

"It's over?" I said.

"Jason…" he began. "Congratulations, Jason."

Dr. Pendergrass believed I'd beat cancer. Chemo was doing more harm than good now. He stopped chemotherapy two months early. Sixteen months and thirty-two rounds of chemotherapy brought me to the end of my fight against cancer. It was the end of the summer of 1992, and my treatment was finishing.

I shook his hand.

"Thank you!"

I jumped for joy on my way out of Bone Tumor Clinic, leaping up and slapping the

A Young Lady, Different from the Rest

top of the examining room's door jam on my way out.

Stepping in the elevator at Children's Hospital, I pressed the "2" button. The elevator door opened a few seconds later and I walked past the room where I had my first treatment; I looked at the three patients curled up in their beds. Passing Erik's room, I looked at the girl who now lay in that bed. I passed the room where I'd said good-bye to Chad, and I looked in at the boy who lay in that bed. And then I walked into the room where I'd have my final treatment.

On that final day of my final treatment, Chappie pulled open the curtain surrounding my hospital bed and sat down next to me.

"How's it feel to be on the victory lap?" he asked.

"Not bad," I answered with a grin.

Chappie opened my file and looked my charts up and down, and then looked up at me.

He closed my file, saying, "Have a safe trip home."

I nodded. "Will I see you soon?" I asked.

"I hope not too soon, Jason," he answered, "I don't think you'll be needing any more surgeries for a while. But send me a postcard or something."

"I will. So long, Chappie."

The sixteen months since I first walked through the doors of Children's Hospital had been full of discovery, agony, and growing up. Friends changed me forever in this place, a place where all different types of miracles happen, if you just take the time to look for them. It had been sixteen months since I truly began to know a God who held me, and even all my problems, in the palm of his hand. My fight against cancer was finished.

I looked through the open curtain that'd surrounded my bed, across the room at a boy leaning over a bucket. I examined his spitting and coughing. His mother held back his dark curly hair, keeping it from falling into his puke. I got up and sat on the end of my bed.

"If you keep your head tipped up, it won't come out of your nose," I said.

The boy turned slowly from his bucket and looked me up and down.

"Thanks," he answered softly.

"Name's Jason," I said. "I'm an expert in the art of throwing up."

PHOTOS
Cancer and Good Friends

Chad practicing his Taekwondo, age 12. Twisp, Washington, 1987.

Jason trying to stay active by playing YMCA basketball. Missoula, Montana, 1992.

Erik and his father, Rick, at a barbeque outside of Children's Hospital. Seattle, Washington, 1991.

Chad and Mom Cherié at Ronald McDonald House. Seattle, Washington, 1991.

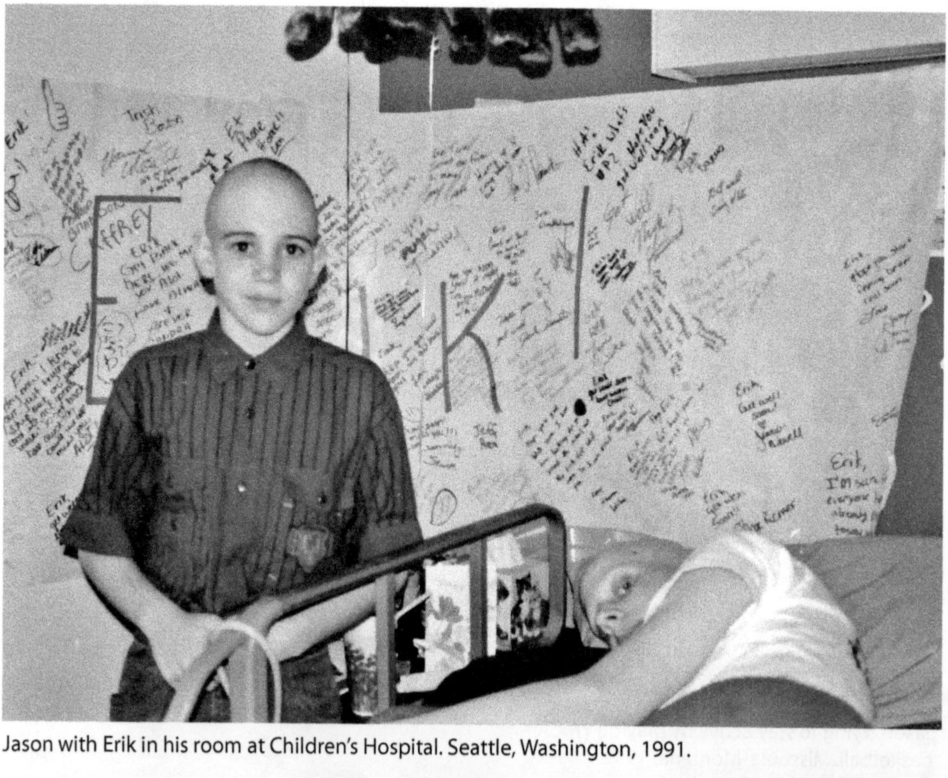

Jason with Erik in his room at Children's Hospital. Seattle, Washington, 1991.

Chad and Jason at the Ronald McDonald House. Seattle, 1991.

Chad, the Junior Prom Prince, spring 1991. Twisp, Washington, 1991.

Chad and Jason with their "Best Friends" T-shirts. Ronald McDonald House, 1991.

Jason fishing on a family trip. Montana, 1992.

Christmas Morning. Missoula, Montana, 1992.

Jason and Jesse. Bellingham, Washington, 1995.

Jason's father, Jeff, Jesse, and Erik's father, Rick. Big Lake, summer, 1993.

Jason and Jesse, 1995.

Jason and Jesse (top right) with her siblings, Kate, Lindsay and Taylor. A visit from the Greers after Carol's breast cancer diagnosis. November, 1995.

Chapter Twenty-Seven

Lighting Strikes, Church Bells Ring, and Our Girl Says Good-bye

Nightmares lost their intensity as time separated me from my cancer and chemotherapy treatments. Finally, they disappeared and were replaced with dreams not so different than those I dreamt before my diagnosis. One dream, similar to a repeating nightmare I used to have, stands out in my memory:

Nothing but black below me... My fingertips are slipping from the cliff's edge; I brace myself for the fall and for my death. I make one last desperate attempt to grab something but to no avail.

I start falling but something stops me—my hand is held by another hand. The hand does not yank me from the edge, it simply catches me. It gives me something to hold on to, a sturdy foundation allowing me to pull myself up.

Kneeling on the steep ground, I catch my breath and then look up to see the face of my savior. But when I lift my head there is no one around. The person who had stood before me is replaced by a light.

My surroundings grow brighter and brighter until I can see for miles in every direction. In the place of my savior, I see the strongest of mountains and warmest of skies, the freshest of grass, and brightest of flowers, the clearest of oceans, whitest of snows. I hear the sounds of singing birds.

* * * * *

I opened my eyes slowly, still sort of wanting to be asleep.

Not jerking awake in the middle of a nightmare, terrified and covered in cold sweat, was an encouraging sign that I was healing. As my body physically healed from the aches and pains of chemotherapy, my emotions and broken heart also healed from losing Chad and Erik. The love of my family, and the families we had grown close to while fighting cancer, had a great deal to do with this healing. In the same way Chad, Erik, Jesse, and I had become friends, I'd also grown close to my friends' parents while fighting cancer. Each of them was genuine and kind, and I knew they loved me right away because they told me so. What's more, if I got in any kind of trouble, I wouldn't just hear about it from Mom. I could count on getting a talking-to by Cherié, Sheri, and Carol.

We all had a connection that was out of the ordinary, special—and we all became part of a great extended family that'd been born at Children's Hospital. I didn't fill in as anyone's new adopted son or sibling after Chad and Erik died. I was more like a smart-alecky nephew who kept on showing up and usually broke something. But my friends' brothers, sisters, and parents all took me in, and seeing them was what I looked forward to most when traveling to Seattle.

I had check-ups at Children's Hospital every three months, and then every six months, and finally a check-up once a year. My hair grew longer and longer with every visit to Seattle. Why did I shy away from a haircut? Why did I have a mop of dark brown, long and somewhat tangled, curly hair? My answer was simple: because I could!

Every check-up at Children's was exactly the same: bone scan, CT scan, blood tests, and then to Bone Tumor Clinic to find out the results from Dr. Pendergrass. The first scan started early in the morning and the appointment at Bone Tumor Clinic would end by six or seven o'clock at night. It was a long day and it never got easier. It didn't matter how long I'd been out of treatment. I held my breath, stomach sunk and sick, hoping, praying that I hadn't relapsed, waiting in suspense for a doctor to give me the news. Thankfully, though almost unbearably, my scans always came back clear at the end of each check-up.

It was rare not to see Chad's, Erik's, and Jesse's families when we were in Seattle. Sometimes Rick and Sheri, or Pat and Carol, would sit in the Children's Hospital waiting room with my parents while I had a scan or blood test. Other times Cherié met us at Chad's and my favorite sports bar to have lunch during a break from the hospital. Oftentimes, especially if it was anywhere near summer, all of us would go stay at Big Lake.

Our visits to Big Lake were fun and warm, spent outside in the water, trying not to get sunburned. Just after Jesse and I finished treatment, we weren't always well enough to go waterskiing or inner-tubing. We'd sit on the ski boat's backseat and just talk while we watched the other kids play.

"Cool, huh? These water toys are the best. Are you gonna try one?" I asked Jesse, who sat next to me in the boat. "Which trick are you gonna do first?"

"Already doing it. I'm just fine right here, relaxing," she said, leaning her head down and looking at me over her dark sunglasses.

Her brown hair was growing fast; long enough to be held back by a headband. She had on a T-shirt that said, "Life's a Peach," and both of us had a few more freckles than usual from spending time outside.

Lighting Strikes, Church Bells Ring, and Our Girl Says Good-bye

"Well, I think you'd be a pretty good slalom skier," I went on. "You could be the only girl ever to land an up-in-the-air somersault, with a twisty thing in the middle. First try, I bet."

"No way," she smiled.

"Well, if you're the first person to do the trick, you'd get to name it probably, just like it was your own invention. You could call it a Do-Hicky, or Thing-a-ma-jig, or the Shoobie-back-Scoobie."

Jesse was laughing now, "I like sitting back and relaxing, okay? And if it was my trick, I certainly wouldn't choose any of those silly names."

Big Lake became one of my favorite places, too. It made me sad that I never visited the lake with Erik. Everybody thought about him and talked about him, though; that's why in my mind, Big Lake was always Erik's Lake. Every so often I'd look at the beach, imagining him as a little kid eating s'mores and looking for pieces of broken glass. I'd try to picture Erik waterskiing as a teenager on the day he found out that he had cancer, and it reminded me why I was growing long hair. Why would you want to go waterskiing first thing after a doctor said you were really sick and needed to take it easy? ...Because you could.

As time passed, Jesse and I got better, stronger, and Erik's brothers soon showed us how to use just about every toy that goes behind a ski boat. Yeah, they even got Jesse out there. There were so many good times at the lake. But it was also there at Big Lake, a couple years after my final chemotherapy treatment, that I heard the most awful news. I was sitting on the dock with Dad, Rick, and Pat. I looked closely at the dads, my father with his beard, Rick and Pat both clean-shaven. Rick was bald on top, and reminded me a lot of Erik. On the other hand, Pat had a thick head of hair, the broad jaw and shoulders of a football player; I'm guessing Jesse and her sisters were glad to be sized more like their mother.

It was an evening on the edge of autumn. The lake wasn't silent. There were the sounds of cars and motorboats, there were shouts and laughs, but each was distanced, hushed by a peace that falls on the water at sunset. Sitting with the dads, my eyes began to follow five sets of footprints, side by side in the sand. Jesse was walking on the shore with all the women: her mom Carol, along with Sheri, Cherié, and my mom. They were talking about the memories that had brought our families together, and deep-down feelings were brought up to the surface to breathe—through teary eyes, they were smiling at each other.

They were too far away for me to actually know what was going on, but Mom told me all about it later. She said they shared funny stories, and they talked about joy, heartbreak, and the worst kind of sadness. They talked about Sheri and Cherié losing their children, and how my mother and Carol were scared because cancer holds on tight, how hard it is to break free from its grasp. But what Mom really needed to explain, what she was getting around to telling me was this: Jesse had relapsed.

"She has two brain tumors this time, son."

Though shocked, I didn't cry and my stomach didn't sink. I wasn't confused or slow in understanding, but right then I knew we were going to lose Jesse, too. The thing that happened was quietness. Not a nice quiet, like sunset on the water, but actual silence. It was like on old war movie: a bomb goes off and a soldier is just standing there, everything drowned out except for a ringing in his ears.

Just like in the movies, the silence only lasted a second or two. I focused in and read Mom's lips until sound came rushing back. Mom told me more about their walk at Big Lake. The three mothers wanted to ask Jesse some questions, to make sure she was all right. Turns out, it was Jesse who ended up making sure the four grown women understood what was going on, what it really is to be "all right" when you're dying.

★ ★ ★ ★ ★

A Look Back: A Love Story

Throughout my life, I have spent time at sea, years if one wanted to log hours aboard one ship or another. The questions of how the ocean and the wind it creates, push a vessel's sails can be studied for a lifetime and still surprise the smart and weathered mariner. I remain a novice, yet the enormous size and mystery of open water lessens my restlessness, and for me, there is a peace while at sea.

When I was new to sailing, a violent storm hit a vessel on which I was a crew member. Its power shook my courage. The captain and each member of the crew pulled tightly together, placing his or her trust in the other. Rain and waves spit at us, wind ripped a hole in our jib, and I think everyone on deck felt some degree of fear. Once the storm passed, the weather calmed, as did the emotions of each person on board. In the calm we began to share stories of one another's lives. I sat with my back against the cold metallic mast, beneath the immense white mainsail that fluttered above us in the now light winds. I spoke briefly about my fight against cancer and about my friend Jesse.

I rarely spoke of cancer, and a dialogue concerning Jesse was even more unusual, as I consider these memories intimate and nearly impossible to describe. It had been several years since I had seen Jesse, but her memory was vivid, and I spoke of her as if we had parted only days before.

My description roused a comment: "Sounds like a love story," the captain said gruffly.

I disagreed, "No, I don't think so."

But when I finally came to a conclusion as to how I would define the nature of Jesse and me, there could be no better description than "a love story."

We shared a depth and closeness while fighting cancer that I have found nowhere else in life. And as my friendships with Chad and Erik differed from those made in Montana while climbing trees, hunting or fishing—my friendship with Jesse was different still. When people of the same gender grow close, they are said to stand shoulder-to-shoulder, and when a girl and boy grow close, they are said to stand face-to-face. In the case of Jesse and me, our differences often appeared to divide us, but ultimately drew us nearer to each other. An awkward and fumbling Jason and a more refined and wise young lady stood amid the same storm, and there we found something that was not clumsy or juvenile, but was chaste, and was truly love.

Matters of the heart have invoked mystery, disappointment, and glee throughout history. I have stumbled in an effort to understand and describe love, and have turned to creation and the Bible for assistance: to God and man, man and woman, Christ and the cross. I have also turned to mythical stories to help realize the love experienced in my life. It is not their facts or historical proof, but the valor, strength, and tragedy of these stories that speak to my heart, even though I don't really understand why.

As I strive to describe the bond between Jesse and me, I am drawn to Homer's well-known Greek myths and to the letters the Apostle Paul wrote to churches in various parts of Greece (while sailing and sometimes finding himself shipwrecked). I am struck by both because as I looked further I learned how, in the Greek language, the complexities of love are not described

Lighting Strikes, Church Bells Ring, and Our Girl Says Good-bye

by one word but by four: Agape, Storge, Philia, and Eros.

Agape is the birth of all love and the beginning of Storge, Philia, and Eros. This is the love between God and mankind, and does not come from our world, but runs through it. It is sometimes hard to see and understand, but Agape courses through our lives every day.

The brush stroke on a celebrated portrait does not reveal the genius of the canvas, but that of the artist. Similarly, if hillsides covered with the thin bowing stems of lavender, or petite blue bouquets of forget-me-nots are not just beautiful themselves, but portray the beauty of their creator, it is Agape that projects this.

Like beauty from a budding hillside, Jesse's patience and kindness were perfect, aged beyond her eleven years, and did not come from, but coursed through her. Jesse conveyed a divine love that magnetically drew me close to her and also closer to God. Perhaps the most peculiar characteristic of Agape is that while other loves take years to develop, this love is often best seen in a child's nature. Jesse's fair skin and darling smile, graceful character, and unshaken faith awed and stirred Agape. I believe that divine love was lent to the world through this sweet girl. Although it is hard to pinpoint the moment when I felt it for first time, I knew how strong and prized this love was when I felt it for the last time.

Jesse was able to live without cancer for more than two years. However, in 1995, Jesse suddenly relapsed. Aggressive tumors again appeared in her brain, and her long battle through cancer ended just after her fifteenth birthday. When she died, it was only fitting that a garden be planted in her memory.

Jesse's Garden was created on the playground of her elementary school in Bellingham, Washington. A small rose-colored fence surrounds it. An arbor of the same color marks the garden's entry. Inside, are her favorite flowers, which included lavender, pansies, forget-me-nots and, of course, a peach tree. A small red-brick path leads to a stone with the engraving: A garden to celebrate the life of Jesse, who taught us how to live, laugh and smell the flowers of life.

I cannot stand among the lavender and forget-me-nots in Jesse's Garden without seeing Agape in their look and fragrance. And I cannot think about the flowers' beauty without remembering how Jesse's life represented the love of Agape.

Storge is often described as the love a parent has for their child. However, as it relates to me and my friendship with Jesse, Storge is not the affection that comes at the beginning of begotten life, but affection for life begotten.

It is not only a love for person, but for places and things. Storge is the love for home and health, sailboats and tea parties. I did not care for tea parties, dolls or perfume, and Jesse did not understand the value a worm has when placed on a fishing hook. Our interests were varied, but our passions fell under the broad category of a life that was loved and worth fighting for to the very end.

Because cancer forced us to realize our days might be cut short, Chad, Jesse, Erik, and I could appreciate a simple joy, and from it, embrace all the possibility, imagination and inviting wonder of a world we had not yet experienced. Each of my friends at Children's Hospital shared a love for little things, forgotten places, and ordinary overlooked gifts. We had in common a love for life, but Jesse and I were able to stay a couple of years longer than the others, able to linger in it together a while after Chad and Erik had gone.

Philia is brotherly or sisterly love and a love between friends. It was the easiest love to detect between Jesse and me. We teased each other often, and were rigid and uncomfortable when asked to embrace for a photograph. We were seldom tender and caring, but warmth arose between us in just the moment it was needed.

In our friendship, Philia was the first love I noticed and the only love I understood at the time. It was virtuous and simple, and it does not surprise me that Philia has been described as the "love between angels."

Eros is a love found in the touch of a hand, a first kiss, and when that one person is found it is the lifelong commitment to intimacy. In the love between Jesse and me, Eros held its breath. The questions of "what if" and "if only" are left to heaven. There is no way to say for sure if Jesse and I would have shared the love of Eros; I can say for sure that she was beautiful, and I can say for sure that our love, like her life, was interrupted.

There is a deep grief for all of those I have loved and lost, and I will carry each of them into every new day. But the sense of loss I have from Jesse's death is different still. It is different because I looked for her in every girl I asked out on a date, and I wondered if she might approve. I think of her scolding finger, and I think of her affirming smile.

The love between a boy and girl is the most difficult for me to understand and describe. We are so different, but our differences somehow allow a love that is unique and many times meant to be shared with a small number of people. Over years, in words, and in study, I cannot adequately describe how much Jesse has meant to me. Part of me is frustrated by this, and part of me is relieved because our love was so precious I want it shared with only few.

* * * * *

I'd been free of cancer for more than two years on the morning of Jesse's memorial service. My hair was long, and my body was stronger and healthier. One of Erik's brothers drove me to the green hillside where Jesse would be buried. By now I was a veteran to cancer and to death, and thought I was going to be strong. I wanted to be. Taking a deep breath, I stepped from the car and held up my head as I walked toward the crowd of people. But when I saw the pastel casket, sized for a child, I froze.

Jesse's mother slipped her hand in mine. "Are you alright, Jason?" Carol asked.

I could just barely hold my tears, so I didn't look at her. Head drooped, staring at the ground, I bit my lip, held my sadness, and answered softly.

"I think so," I replied.

But then there was a hand on my shoulder, then another, and another. I looked up. Along with Carol, I now saw Jesse's father, Erik's mother and father, Chad's mother, my mother and father. I looked at each face, those who had experienced the greatest possible loss, circled around me. Again, my head drooped and Carol grasped my hand more firmly. And when I looked toward my hand and hers, I saw the silver of Grandpa Greer's ring wrapped around my pinky. And in the squeeze of Carol's hand, I saw an identical ring that my grandfather had made for Jesse before she died, now on Carol's little finger.

I bit my lip again and looked back up at those around me. I thought of the journey, the suffering we had all been through together—it was kind of hard to define where one family ended and another began. There was no more holding on to my sadness. It welled up and spilled over. My vision blurred as tears streamed down my cheeks. My legs began to quake and my knees started to buckle, but I was held up by my parents and the parents of my friends.

When Jesse's casket was put into the ground, I thought of the final days of her life. I remembered that her blood cells were low and platelets almost non-existent. She was bleeding a lot from her nose and mouth. If she coughed, sneezed, or even breathed

Lighting Strikes, Church Bells Ring, and Our Girl Says Good-bye

very hard at all, the oxygen mask covering her mouth would splatter with blood. One time, Mom reached over to adjust Jesse in the hospital bed and clean out the mask. Mom was timid, afraid she'd hurt her somehow.

"It's all right, you can do this," Jesse had coached my mother.

Mom and Dad were at the hospital, but they weren't next to Jesse when she died. Dad had made a kids' tent out of extra bed sheets and couch cushions in the hospital waiting room. He and Mom were crouching inside the tent with Jesse's brother and sisters. They were keeping the girls company and looking at a picture book with Jesse's younger brother.

Pat and Carol were alone with their daughter during her final seconds, and when they later shared the story with the rest of us, I memorized the description and every detail forever seared my memory. I could think of nothing else as Jesse's casket inched lower and lower into the ground.

In my mind, I could see blood falling from her nose and mouth as she lay in her hospital bed. A lightning storm was filling the sky, a display that Pat later called *phenomenal*. And then suddenly, unexpectedly, church bells were ringing. I could picture Jesse's mother and father leaning over her bed. They were both kissing her on opposite cheeks at the exact same time, amid the lightning and ringing bells, and it was then, in those moments of a kiss and the crash of sound, that Jesse left our world.

I flashed back to Mom's story of their conversation at Big Lake, that day when Jesse walked with all the moms along the lake's shoreline. Jesse was going to die, and the women wanted to make sure she was all right. They had questions and they thought they had some explanations, but it was Jesse who had *the* answer.

"Well, when it's our time...on the day when we die, Jesus will be waiting there for us," Carol had reassured her daughter.

Jesse had stopped walking and looked up at her mother.

Jesse's voice had been absolutely certain, her faith so pure, in her answer: "You know, he really will be, Mom."

And then my mother had had a question. "Jesse," she asked, "are you angry at God for allowing your tumors to be in remission for a short time, only to relapse again?"

Once more, Jesse's answer had come without wavering, without doubt.

"How could I be? I've been given all of this extra time."

A gentle thump rose from the ground as Jesse's casket settled into the soil at the bottom of her gravesite. I stood there on the grassy hillside, legs no longer quaking but tears still streaming steadily. My vision blurred as I looked down at her pastel casket, now snugly tucked into a small rectangular hole in the earth.

Jesse was gone. So were Erik, Chad, even Travis, my fellow Montanan whom I'd known for barely a few weeks at the beginning of treatment. All dead. I was the only one left. I felt the familiar grief, the pang of ache from *another* final good-bye, wrestling with God and asking, "Who am I to be the one privileged to live?" My questions twisted around heartbreaking emotions, they tangled together, and wound tightly into a knot; cold and gray, confusing and heavy they sank deep within me.

While still at the foot of death, just steps from Jesse's grave, I also began to feel something else. Like the bells' chime in the last seconds of her life, there was a ringing of hope. In the face of grief and because of it, I felt something rising up inside, expanding, filling that gray place with one clear understanding: I was also so thankful for the extra time God had given me.

It may be that only beside death, when suffering and loss are raw and real, that we can understand the preciousness of living. In that moment, more than any other, I was truly grateful for the gift of those warm childhood days in Montana, for the days spent alongside those young, quiet heroes with whom I'd fought cancer, and for the gift of days still to come.

I wiped my tears with the back of my hand and drew in a deep, ragged breath. And when I finally walked away from Jesse's grave, I was looking ahead, less with fear, or the guilt of surviving dear friends, but further bestowed with a responsibility to squeeze the most out of every heartbeat, breath, and moment. I looked ahead, welcoming the unknown, the rest of my life and all its mystery.

Epilogue

I would sacrifice anything to give back the children to the parents who circled me at Jesse's grave. I would give anything to erase the look a parent's face takes once they have lost a child. However, as for my life, my scars are a badge; I have been tested and I am stronger. My life never returned to the childhood in which I lived before cancer, my place in life was never again the same—it was better.

Often I think of lying in the hospital during my first chemotherapy treatment and noticing those lines on my Grandma Dorie's face. Today, my face also has lines left from long smiles and from hard times: both remind me of a grand romance.

I have experienced graduations and a professional career, had my blood warmed by bourbon, and heard a six-string guitar played to perfection from a smoky stage. I have seen love's surrender reflected in the eyes of a woman, held the helm of a ship as the equator passed beneath me, and felt the spin of a wrench under the hood of a 1957 Chevrolet.

From horizon to horizon and from sea to peak, sight and sound, feel and flavor, all romances me. The softest colors of twilight rising for their fifteen minutes of fame every morning and every evening, the dive of a gull and the breach of a whale, the might of crashing mountains and the gentleness of a rising mist, the depths of the ocean and an orchard of stars, the cry of a newborn baby—these are the very thoughts of God.

But this is only half of the story, only part of the romance. There is hate, death, cruelty, and selfishness. Tragedy is in the sway of every day, and for me, cancer was but a baptism into the difficulties life holds. The groan of heartbreak did not end with chemotherapy. However, more than anything else, cancer has shown me that the lines left by long smiles are not always in spite of imperfect circumstance, many times they can be found because of imperfection and difficulty, because of the lines left by hard times: beauty is not only found in ease or fair weather, it is also found in the bumps and chop, it is found in the storms.

My fight against cancer stripped me of comforts and brought me to my knees. It made me question Christianity. It gave me grief, loneliness, and mortal fear. But without fear, I would have no courage, and without my sickness, I could not appreciate my health. Without being close to death, I would have no urgency to live life. My fight cut through shallow friendship and gave me deep communion among those with whom I suffered. It cut through religion and gave me a deep and intimate faith. Without cancer, I may have never realized the romance—life is full of wonder and beauty, it is reckless and wild, it is not *safe*, but it is *good*.

Cancer is a murdering disease of the most politically correct nature; it does not discriminate against age or race, sex, or religion. The disease kills men and women, young and old, black and white, Christian, Jewish, Muslim, and atheists, and has done so for centuries. Fighting cancer is a bitter and difficult battle. But if I could be so bold, I say, "Though cancer is certainly *a* fight, it is not *the* fight." I believe with all of my heart that the fight is not to avoid dying. I believe the fight is to be truly alive. Cancer is one circumstance, one errand runner for death. If all mankind has one thing in common, it is communion in suffering, and finally mortality. The greatest tragedy is not death, but the death of desire while a heart still beats.

After my final chemotherapy treatment, I had tried to callus my heart and turn away from cancer, but I could not; closing my eyes to this disease did not make it disappear. And so, after a few years of trying to close myself off from the world of cancer and chemotherapy, I finally dove headlong into the lives of children fighting the same disease that I had years before.

It was very near my seventeenth birthday when I walked into the Children's Hospital, not as a patient, but as a spectator of someone else's fight. I stepped out of the elevator on the second floor, and the sight and scent evoked so many poignant memories of being a patient that I became ill, and I was forced to find a bathroom so I could throw up. When I regained my composure enough to leave the bathroom, I sat in a chair next to the child I had come to visit, both of us nauseous, both holding a similar expression, and a friendship began.

The boy I visited was ten years old, and reminded me much of the child I was when I fought cancer. When I was diagnosed, I was just a little older than he. His cancer was similar to mine, and his eyes were innocent and filled with wonder. Following our introduction and beginning of our friendship, I walked with him through his fight, and I walked with him to his death.

One afternoon I stood with him at the end of his young life, and as he looked up at me, he asked, "Jason, will I die?"

After a few moments of silence I knelt down next to his hospital bed and asked him to hold out his hands.

The boy held out his hands. Then I asked the boy to wiggle his fingers, and he did. Then, willing the tears from my eyes, I said, "If you can wiggle your fingers, you can make a fist. If you can make a fist, there's still fight in you."

Kneeling next to that ten-year-old boy's hospital bed, I silently prayed and asked God for a miracle. It was not the miracle I had prayed for Erik, Chad, Jesse, or what I would have prayed for this boy in the past. I did not ask God to reach down and take this boy's cancer from him. Divine healing was not my request. I prayed for an exchange of life—mine for his. Once again I held my breath and closed my eyes, and for the first time I asked God to allow me to take this child's place.

My request was not answered; my miracle was not delivered. I wrote the benediction for the little boy's memorial service. He was the first child since Chad, Erik, and Jesse that I was brave enough to care for, but was not the last. He was the first child I asked to hold out his hands, wiggle his fingers, and make a fist; he was not the last. As this ten-year-old-boy approached his death, for the first time I asked God to let me take the place of a sick child, and I have asked this of God several times since. The benediction I wrote for his memorial service was my first. Sadly, it was not my last.

Epilogue

Since the day I walked into Children's Hospital and again opened my heart to others who fought cancer, I have been involved in organizations and summer camps, hospitals, and McDonald Houses. Frequently, however, an introduction to a child fighting cancer has not come from any hospital or non-profit organization. It often comes through a phone call from a scared parent or patient.

I cannot claim to have been involved in the lives of a large number of children fighting cancer. Rather, I have been blessed with a few cherished friendships. Yet, nearly every year since my diagnosis, a child close to me has died of cancer. Knowing these children has been the greatest joy of my life, and losing them has been my life's great anguish. The wound that I carry as I walk through life, while walking others to their death, is a wound that is too deep for me to heal. There is nothing I can ever do to justify why I live and other children die of cancer. There is nothing I can ever do to make right the fact that my flawed character remains, while others who seem to have the constitution of angels pass away.

There is nothing I can ever do, so I pour my wound into the wounds in the hands and feet of a crucified Christ—I give to God what I cannot change or heal. Giving my wound away does not magically heal grief or suddenly answer the questions of "Why?" However, deep cries out to deep. In my deep wounds and in the deep wounds of Christ I am given a communion of suffering, camaraderie with my savior because we have both bled and wept. I surrender to wounds deeper than mine, to a crucifixion that somehow makes right what I cannot. And I surrender to a grand plan of which I can see only a small part of, and do not understand.

Pouring the wounds left from participating in these children's lives into the wounds of Christ provides me with an understanding of the "grace" spoken of by my father when I was young. I do not deserve one day of the life I have been fortunate enough to live. Just as I do not deserve the deep and intimate faith I enjoy each day, or the eternity that awaits once my life has finished. These are a gift, beyond what I can earn or deserve. It is simply grace—and I accept it.

Without the gift of grace the weight of living in the midst of death would cause me to break. I could not give my heart recklessly to others knowing full well that at some point it will be broken. Without grace I could not endure a life of both deep love and loss. I could not live a life so laced with sweetness and joy, as well as bitterness and grief.

With the gift of grace I can confidently say: bring me the sweet, bring me the bitter, but leave the bland for another. Bring me the deep love, bring me the deep wound, but leave the shallow for another. Bring me the fluttering heart, bring me the broken heart, but leave the cowardice of never loving for another. With grace and certainty borrowed from my friend Jesse, I will remain grateful for this extra time, forever trying to live *deeply* and *love recklessly, until it hurts.*

When it does hurt, when I am again in the center of loss, in the midst of that beautiful missing that only comes after truly caring, in those last days when I am privileged to catch a glimpse of something holy as young friends pass on, warning me that I have silently edged a bit closer to my own mortality—still, hope remains. It is then that I think most about Erik raising his hands toward heaven, gone instantly without pain. Then I am reminded of "The Three Musketeers," as Chad called us, and the last thing he said to me: "I'll be watching for you." I am thankful for my life, gratefully awake to all the romance, but am also curious for that next adventure. I am pulled between those who I love here and the friends and Jesus waiting for me. Wondering where my life will lead and when it will end, where my tiny piece fits into God's plan and if it is somehow meant to fit alongside children still in cancer's awful grip, it is then that I am drawn to the Apostle Paul's writing in Philippians 1:23-24: *But I am hard-pressed from both directions, having the desire to depart and be with Christ, for that is very much better; yet to remain on in the flesh is more necessary for your sake.*

PHOTOS
Very Much Better

Jason and his parents, Deb and Jeff. Montana, 2004.

Dad and boys aboard the *Keshia Dawn*, southeast Alaska. (Left: 1982, right, 2003.)

Christmas Day campfire. Jon and Jason with parents, Deb and Jeff. Missoula, Montana, 2004.

The "moms", Cherié, Carol, Mom Deb, Sheri. Bellingham, Washington, 2004.

The "dads" at Big Lake, Rick, Pat, and Dad. Big Lake, 1995.

Jason, commercial fishing in Bristol Bay, Alaska, 2002.

Jason and Emily Greer engagement party. Big Lake, Washington, 2006.

She said "YES" on Big Lake. From left: Grandma Dorie, Jason's parents, Jason and his wife, Emily, Emily's dad, Grandpa Harp. Big Lake, 2006.

Jason and Emily Greer at their wedding. Hamilton, Montana, 2007.

Jason as a camp counselor: "Velcro Man" at pediatric cancer camp, Camp Agape Northwest. Gig Harbor, Washington, 2002.

Jason volunteering as a counselor at Camp Agape Northwest. Gig Harbor, Washington, 2002.

A Final Note

Letters to Heaven

Alone in silence, with memories I waltz: I step back to a time past, then grab a hold and step forward. It is a sound, a scent, a photograph that take me back and steal my breath. I wish that I did not *remember* those lost in my life, because I wish that I would never, not for a moment, *forget* them. But even when the memory of a friend has not overwhelmed me, I carry these people with me—all of them.

Words are used to describe memories, and when described properly, memories can almost breathe life. Adjectives and verbs sometimes seem to bring missed laughs, voices, or embraces alive once again. The many words of this story describe antiquities, dusted off moments past, the kiss of reminiscence, a part of my life gone forever but remembered in vivid, and seemingly present, detail. Remembering and writing this story brought near to me friends who have passed away, made them alive again in my mind and in my heart. But always there is a final chapter, page, word, a final punctuation—and the loved are lost once again.

When I write of my life, I believe intently in heaven. And sometimes I feel as though friends who have died are so close that the laws of time and death are absent. Sometimes it feels like sending a letter to a time in the past or to heaven is entirely possible.

Regardless of feeling, words cannot find their way to yesterday through a letter in H.G. Wells' time machine, and probably will not be delivered by the hands of God. But, if only for a moment, writing or reading about a loved one can draw them near. And if done wholeheartedly, just as our prayers are heard, maybe the words in a letter could also find their way to heaven, especially in those moments when heaven feels close, and death and time feel absent.

So letters to Erik, Chad, and Jesse have been written, as if they could be folded, tucked into an envelope and sent to heaven. Because only a mother can truly describe the love of a mother, and a father, the love of a father, Rick and Sheri, Cherié, and Pat and Carol have written to their children. Their children's faith in life and death is miraculous, magic, and meant to be sung. So, too, these letters are meant to be read wholeheartedly in the hope that the words might somehow leave the pages of this memoir and find their way to heaven.

* * * * *

To our precious son Erik,

Thank you, Erik, for the joy and laughter you brought into our lives from the moment you were born. You were such a big, healthy baby – 9 lbs., 5 oz. Your brothers adored you. You were born on our 7th wedding anniversary; from then on our anniversary celebrations always involved little boys and birthday parties! Even today, August 30th remains bittersweet. We remember your first day home from the hospital…it was so hot at the end of August that we had the front door open with you laying on the couch while we ate dinner. After cleaning up in the kitchen, we walked into the living room to find you missing. You cannot imagine the panic that we felt. But you were safely upstairs in your cradle in our bedroom. Your young brothers had carried you up the steps all by themselves and put you in your bed. We never quite wanted to picture how that took place, but were so relieved to see you safely sleeping in your cradle with your proud brothers standing by your side. You never knew a moment that wasn't filled with love.

You were so bright; so intelligent. You could read the newspaper by the time you were three years old in preschool. You were a whiz at spelling. Remember the spelling bees? You made Dad and I so proud every step of your life. Of course, you were a challenge, too! Dad and I used to joke with each other about the best way to deal with a child who could outsmart us! We love to tell the story of the night we kept tucking you into bed and you kept sneaking back downstairs. We had already done the one more story, the one more prayer, the one more drink. You were actually very close to getting a spanking when you hopped up on the couch between us and put your arms around our shoulders and said that with such a large family, this was the only "quality time" you had with your parents. You were probably only 4 years old. Needless to say, we spent "quality time" together with you that evening and many evenings after that, and are so glad that we did.

Every memory fills our eyes with tears, but every memory also fills our hearts with joy. We remember all of our travels. You had such a passion for history. You wanted to be a lawyer and then President of the United States…President at least up to the time we visited John F. Kennedy's library. You didn't want to die young. While we were touring, you always had a book with you, studying and learning everything you could about the places we visited. You were such an avid reader, such an enthusiastic student. We remember you telling us that an "A" was like a "B" to you; an "A-" like a "C;" only "A+'s" pleased you. Did you put too much pressure on yourself? Did we? We didn't want you to experience stress; we only wanted you to enjoy life. When we write "enjoy life," we have to say that we have never known anyone who enjoyed life more, or for that matter lived life more wholeheartedly than you. That comforts us. Your life may not have been long, but it was definitely lived to the fullest.

We learned so much from you, Erik. We learned to live our lives to the fullest…to enjoy every moment that we have…to take the tough things in stride and to smile and laugh through them. We trusted God with your life from the moment you were born and trusted

A Final Note

Erik and family: (back row) Erik, (center, left to right) Rick and Sheri, (front row, left to right), Geoff, Jonathan, Ryan. Big Lake, Washington, 1990.

Him throughout your battle with cancer. Although initially, I must admit, I tried to help God. I told Him I had a better plan. I told Him that if He healed you, so many people would come to believe in Him. Then as your diagnosis got tougher, I said to God, "Oh, I see what you are doing. If you had healed Erik right away, people would think that he never really had cancer. I get it! Now with cancer in the last stage, when Erik is healed, people will truly believe in Your power." But very quickly we came to the point where we totally relied on God. We knew that He loved and cared for you even more than we did and we trusted that He would hold you in His mighty arms and shield you from pain and death.

Speaking of death, your death was the most incredibly beautiful thing we have ever witnessed in our entire lives. We thought that the day you were born was the most awesome miracle we would ever experience, but your death was a miracle, too.

Remember how we read Romans 5:1-5 over and over again while you were in the hospital? Therefore, since we are justified by faith, we have peace with God through our Lord Jesus Christ. Through him we have obtained access to this grace in which we stand, and we rejoice in our hope of sharing the glory of God. More than that, we rejoice in our sufferings, knowing that suffering produces endurance, and endurance produces character, and character produces hope, and hope does not disappoint us, because God's love has been poured into our hearts through the Holy Spirit which has been given to us.

What we had in mind in the "hope" was healing, but God definitely did not disappoint us. Moments after you died, the whole family sat in a room together and I read Romans 5 again and for the first time we saw that you were whole and healthy – more whole and healthy than you had ever been in your life and you had obtained that hope of sharing the glory of God.

Now in church when we sing "I Rejoiced the Day You Were Baptized," those words are so meaningful to us. God truly was there with "just one last surprise" for you. We saw the look on your face. We experienced a glimpse of Heaven through your eyes. The words you shared with us – words that we realized later came straight from Jesus – comfort us still today.

We remember how your doctors and Pastor Gene said that they had never seen anyone die with more dignity and faith. They said that they had never heard the words, "I love you" or "I am so proud of you" heard more times than in your room. Your witness and your story have traveled all over the world. We thank God every day for His gift of faith and peace.

We remain so proud of you and so happy for you. We realized after your death that you had attained the ultimate goal that we pray for and wish for our children – you were in Heaven with your Heavenly Father. Our prayer for our sons has always been that they would love the Lord with all their hearts and souls and might, serve God and walk humbly with their Lord and Savior.

Remember the pact you had us make with all of our hands together right before you died…to live our lives so that we could all join you in Heaven. Dad and I pray daily for the Holy Spirit to guide us and give us the strength to do that. Your brothers have grown up. They married beautiful women who have brought us such joy. You have three beautiful nephews and a niece who have helped to fill the empty place that your death left in our hearts. You always wanted to have a large family. We will be excited to see what is happening with you in Heaven. When people ask us, "When does the grief and pain go away?," we say that you died 15 years ago, so all we know is that it takes longer than that. We miss you every single day, but the piercing pain that your death left in our lives has softened.

Of course, what are we telling you all this for, you promised to be watching over us. Thank you for that gift. Thank you for giving us permission to go on living and having fun. We could not have done that without your gracious encouragement.

We will love you forever. The words from II Timothy 4:7 that are written on your gravestone describe your life for us… "I have fought the good fight. I have finished the race. I have kept the faith." We pray that we can follow the example you set for us and look forward with great joy to being reunited with you in Heaven.

With all our love,
Dad and Mom

* * * * *

To my dear son Chad, October 20, 2005
You fought the good fight,
You finished the race,
You kept the Faith…

It has been fourteen years today that the Lord relieved you from your pain of cancer and took you to his heavenly home.

Chad, you were God's gift to me for 16 years and 7 months. I am so very blessed that you were my son, blessed by the way God molded your special character. With your wonderful smile, the love in your heart, and your sense of humor you touched many hearts in a mighty positive way. I often hunger for your keen sense of humor. I just smile when I think of it. The pain is not as severe as it was the first few years you were gone. I focus on the joy you

A Final Note

brought into my life. As tough as life can be sometimes, your strength, your courage, and how you embraced each and every day has encouraged me to be strong, and keep the faith so that I can accomplish what I need to while I am here on earth.

    I thank you for watching over your brother Bill from heaven, and giving him the strength to persevere in his life and recognize the goodness in his heart. He feels you have been his guardian angel and so do I. Now he is a Daddy to a beautiful little girl, Mackenzie Mae. She is a positive light in his every day. You would absolutely enjoy Mackenzie, you had such a creative mind and so does Mackenzie. Your little niece is a loving, caring child of God. I am proud to be her Grandmother.

    Since you had so much fun with your Radio Controlled Truck, I thought you would like to know that your high school classmate Tobey has it and he and his son really enjoy running it around. I was pleased to hear about that, just last summer. Tobey told me he was so happy to have it.

Chad, I Love You and I will always miss you. Thanks for the memories.
Love, Your Mother
Cherié
P.S. Hug your grandmother for me.

Family portrait. Chad, four years old, and Bill, eight years old. 1979.

* * * * *

Fall 2006

    My dearest Jesse,
    I miss you. Despite believing and knowing you are in heaven being loved in a way that is incomprehensible to me, with a beautiful, perfect love, I want you here, next to me...still. I want to see the corners of your eyes crinkle when you laugh. I want to make a pot of tea and cut out paper dolls all afternoon, even though I know if you were still here that's probably not what we'd be doing. I miss your gentle smile and the way your eyes lit up when you gave a gift. When I garden I think of you and all the flowers you loved; bleeding hearts, fairy roses,

Jesse's family: Mom and Dad, Pat and Carol; Jesse (bottom right), Kate (bottom center), Lindsay (bottom left); Carol is holding baby Taylor. Jesse is enjoying a short remission and the family is on vacation in Grandview, Washington. July, 1990.

lavender, and especially pansies because they have faces. Remember the silver vase you bought for me at the hospital? You made me wait outside even though you could hardly walk after the transplant, then, you paid them some thirty dollars in quarters you had stashed. We got to the room and you were exhausted. You couldn't wait much beyond the door of our room to give me my present. I always fill that vase with peonies in the spring.

I miss the daily experience of your love. It was never to be the love of an adult daughter, bride or new mother, but it was a love that did not remember my mistakes or tally wrongs. Your love was a pure, unconditional love. It was the love of a lifetime in a condensed and accelerated season.

I am thankful for the many miracles we experienced in our cancer years. God's love and mercy were continually displayed in the many ways He assured us of His presence, right there in the midst of bald heads, hospitals, endless tests and throw-up. When I was diagnosed with breast cancer, I thought we'd go to heaven together, or maybe I'd go and you'd be healed, able to spend more years with Dad, Lindsay, Kate and Taylor. My plans were not His, however, and after your death, in my grief He assured me still that your life was complete as He planned it, and He delighted in you.

Our days were written in His book before the foundation of the world.

I miss you my Jesse, but I wait patiently, knowing He has appointed my days, and then I will see you again. I know you'll be waiting for me—for all of us.

We love you so much,
Mom and Dad
And your sisters and brother

* * * * *

A Final Note

It is today, reflecting upon the advancements of the past, in this century, in my generation, that we stand on the cusp of a cure. Genius is the place where intellect and passion meet eye to eye, and this is the place where the killer called *cancer* will be stopped. Humanity has not relented in striving to understand the world where we have been placed, unlocking the secrets of creation. Please continue working and discovering so that we might silence a piper that has already stolen too many of our children, cure cancer, and have no more lost to this disease.

— *Jason Paul Greer*

Resources

American Cancer Society, Inc., "Chemotherapy: What It Is, How It Works." *American Cancer Society* May 15, 2008 (2002). http://www.cancer.org/docroot/ETO/content/ETO_2x_Chemotherapy_What_It_Is_How_It_Helps.asp>.

American Cancer Society, Inc., "The History of Cancer." *American Cancer Society* May 15, 2008. (2002) http://www.cancer.org/docroot/CRI/content/CRI_2_6x_the_history_of_cancer_72asp.

Gandt, Lois, ed., *A Century of Oncology: a Photographic History of Cancer Research and Therapy*. Greenwich: Greenwich, 1997.

Kullendorff, Carl-Magnus, Fredrik Mertens, Mikael Donner, Thomas Wieb, Maus Akerman, and Nils Mandahl. "Cytogenic Aberations in Ewings Sarcoma: are Secondary Changes Associated with Clinical Outcome?" *Medical and Pediatric Oncology* 32 (1999): 79-83.

Lewis, C.S. *The Lion, the Witch, and the Wardrobe*. San Francisco: HarperCollins, 1988.

Lewis, C.S. *The Four Loves*. San Diego: A Harvest Book Harcourt, Inc., 1988.

MacLean, Norman. *A River Runs Through It: And Other Stories by Norman Maclean*. Chicago: The University of Chicago, 1976.

Rilke, Rainer. *Diaries of a Young Poet*. New York: W.W. Norton & Company, Inc., 1998.

Rilke, Rainer. *Letters to a Young Poet*. New York: W.W. Norton & Company, Inc., 1998.

Chicago formatting by BibMe.org.

www.ingramcontent.com/pod-product-compliance
Lightning Source LLC
Chambersburg PA
CBHW051057160426
43193CB00010B/1214